THE FAMOUS YORKSHIREMEN:
THE FORGOTTEN HISTORY OF REDCAR'S FOOTBALLING PIONEERS

An Old Bird Publishing book

www.redcarfootball.com

Copyright © Thomas Neal, 2021

The moral right of the author has been asserted. All rights reserved. Without limiting the rights under copyright restricted above, no part of this publication may be reproduced, stored in or introduced into a retrieval system, or transmitted, in any form of by any means (electronic, mechanical, photocopying, recording or otherwise), without the prior written permission of the copyright owner.

Every effort has been made to trace or contact all copyright holders. The publishers will be pleased to make good any omissions or rectify any mistakes brought to their attention at the earliest opportunity.

1st Edition 2021, paperback

ISBN: 978-1-3999-0699-9

Front and back cover designed by Steven Renney

Edited by Martin Neal

The Famous Yorkshiremen:
The Forgotten History of Redcar's Footballing Pioneers

By Tom Neal

Contents

Author's Notes	9
Prologue	11
Beginnings	13
Competition	25
Forces Divided	35
Loss	50
Custodians	58
Challenges	71
A New Era	100
Invincible	112
The Modern Age	125
Epilogue	135
Select Details	137
Acknowledgements	142
References	144

For Isla and Milo

And for Katie

Author's Notes

Back in April 2020, during the first Coronavirus lockdown, I put together a two-page document for Redcar Athletic Football Club to use as a reference for some social media posts. They wanted to tell some interesting stories about the history of football in the town, and I'd done some basic research using newspapers, online articles and journals to piece together a few interesting titbits.

A short while later, as the 2020/21 season drew nearer, the club reached out to ask what my regular programme article would be about this year. I had written some "snapshots" in the previous season's programme about that week's opponents, mainly making bad puns and references to TV shows that no-one watches. I'd run out of material by the end of the season, and there's only so many times you can mention the fact that West Allotment is alleged to have the largest conglomeration of purpose-built office space in the Northern Hemisphere.

That's when I thought about writing about the history of football in Redcar. I'd already made a bit of a head start and I found it fascinating, so why not? I put this idea to Redcar Athletic chairman Kev Fryett, who was enthusiastic but sceptical. "Honestly Tom, football history in Redcar is a real struggle," he told me. That was when I'd definitely made my mind up.

After yet more curtailments thanks to the pandemic, I found myself two seasons in with only a handful of articles gone to print. There was no chance I was going to let all that hard work go to waste, which is why this book is here today.

•

A note about the geography of the area, because although many readers will be more than familiar with the towns and districts of Redcar and Cleveland, it should not be assumed that everyone is. Redcar is a town situated on the North East coast, just under eight miles east of Middlesbrough. The town has gone through many changes in the last couple of centuries and now encompasses many areas that were once separate; from Coatham and Warrenby in the north, Lazenby in the east and Kirkleatham in the south.

Its close proximity to other north eastern towns like Middlesbrough, Saltburn, Marske, Guisborough, Eston and South Bank saw Redcar's rise inexorably linked to theirs, as the industrial revolution changed the face of Teesside forever. These towns have also shared links on the football field for as long as a ball has been kicked there, so Redcar's travels to their local rivals have long been a talking point in the town. It is not necessary to know exactly where these towns are in the region, just that they have been there for as long as - or longer than - Redcar has been, and that passionate local pride is rarely far away when it comes to sporting events in the North East.

●

If I can speak for a moment about the title itself, it may be the cause of some contention. That's because Redcar, although historically part of North Yorkshire, is now part of the unitary authority of Redcar and Cleveland, and not technically part of any county. The title *'The Famous Yorkshiremen'* comes from a colourful article in the now-defunct publication *The Athletic News*, speaking about the prestige of the Redcar team as they faced Small Heath Alliance, now Birmingham City, in the FA Cup. I liked this moniker as it suggested that Redcar were not only famous in Teesside, or even North Yorkshire, but the huge part of the country that makes up Yorkshire itself.

It should also be noted that this book is not, nor does it claim to be, a definitive account of every football team in Redcar. Instead, it aims to tell the story of the town's relationship with the game throughout the years, and how certain clubs and players left an indelible mark on the sport in their own unique ways. There are many teams rarely mentioned that readers may have fond memories of; Redcar Park Rangers, Redcar Blue Star, Redcar Parish Church, Redcar Spartans, Redcar Sacred Heart and Redcar Victoria to name a few. Instead, the book focuses on stories that have rarely been told, bringing new information to light that has been lost to time since their first publication, some of them over 140 years ago.

Tom Neal
London, 2021

Prologue

1847.

In the shadow of Huntcliff, a man pushes his feet across the sandy shore of Saltburn beach. The sun hangs low in the autumn sky, its light dancing on the gentle waves of the North Sea. He makes his way south, towards the village of Skinningrove, looking for something. There are indentations in the sand that have been left behind by orange rocks taken away by small craft that moor on the beach at high water to bring them back to Tyneside. The indentations are filled with seawater, turned a deep orange hue by the iron oxide. These ironstone deposits are valuable, especially since those found elsewhere in County Durham and Grosmont have been found to be inadequate in both quantity and quality.

"What are you looking for?" asks an approaching man.

"Some men in my employ gather ironstone from this beach", replies the seeker, "I was looking for more as they have cleared it all from Saltburn."

"I have something very like that on my property, would you object to coming to take a look?" comes the reply.

The property belongs to Anthony Lax Maynard, a landowner from nearby Skinningrove. The other man, Samuel Okey, is an ore collector who at once proceeds to Maynard's land to discover for himself if what he said was true. It was. What the two men had discovered would come to be known as the Cleveland Main Seam and its discovery would change the area forever.

Over the course of the next few years, mines and furnaces opened all around Cleveland in what would be dubbed the "Great Iron Rush". By 1862, Chancellor and future Prime Minister William Gladstone visited the ironworks and famously described the new town of Middlesbrough – whose population had exploded from 5,000 to 19,000 in just 10 years – as an "Infant Hercules". By 1871 there were over 100 furnaces punctuating the River Tees between Stockton and Redcar, with Middlesbrough – the great Ironopolis – now a town of 40,000.

By the time 1876 rolled around, Middlesbrough was a working class powerhouse. Coupled with the fact that they had unions to fight for reasonable working hours, employees at the steelworks needed – and now had time for - a pastime. Luckily for them, the local cricketers needed something to keep them busy during the winter months, and watching what the locals at South Bank had been getting up to for the past few years, it was agreed (not over a tripe supper, as originally thought) to form Middlesbrough Football Club, and play under the association rules.

Sheffield had already paved the way for football in the North, taking the rules formally used by Old Boys in affluent southern areas of the country and forming their own rules to share with the northern working classes in the 1850s and '60s. The booming steel industry was driving people to Teesside from all over the country, and with them came the Beautiful Game. It didn't take long for other towns to follow Middlesbrough's lead, with Eston, Whitby and Loftus joining South Bank to bring more widespread and competitive football to the area.

This is where Redcar comes in. Until the 19th century, the town was much smaller than those that surrounded it. The town, nestled between the Guisborough hills and the North Sea, was a sub-parish of the nearby Marske-by-the-Sea and it regularly traded with larger nearby towns such as Coatham, which appears in the Domesday Book in 1066 alongside Marske. After Redcar became a fashionable destination for Victorian holidaymakers, the town's economy boomed and it eventually swallowed up nearby areas which became districts of Redcar.

As was the case in Middlesbrough, despite the growing working class population that would eventually come to build an affinity with the game, football arrived in many northern towns from the public school Old Boys via the middle classes and not from the working man. A growing economy in the area meant more need for teachers, accountants and engineers. Their involvement with the local cricket clubs meant they were first in line to feature for the football clubs they helped to form.

As Redcar began to find itself benefitting from the boom in the area initially instigated by the iron rush, its middle classes would also find themselves looking for something to do in the wintertime...

Chapter 1: Beginnings

In a cramped home tucked away in the Cambridgeshire countryside in the middle of the 19th century, James Howcroft was born. The youngest child of a large family, by the time he was nine, through a mix of his eldest siblings leaving the nest and the tragedy of some of the younger ones passing away, the Howcroft family home in the market town of Wisbech had reduced to four; James, his brother Hugh who was one year his senior, 19-year-old Joseph who had followed in his father's footsteps to become a butcher, and his mother Sarah, a seamstress originally from Norfolk. Ten years later, he found himself far from home, living with his mother in Dalston, London, and in order to support his unemployed mother, the teenaged James was forced to grow up quickly. To pay the bills, he found work as a builder's clerk, and it would set him up for a lifelong career when he would move to Redcar a few years later. Unbeknownst to him, his move to the north east coast would see him achieve far more than a good career; not only making history as a footballer, but changing the game itself.

James Howcroft
Sports Gazette, 13th April 1912

Howcroft was a stocky young man, "yeoman-built,"[1] with a ruddy complexion and jet black hair that would turn white in his later age. His experiences at home in Cambridgeshire and London would go on to serve him well in later life; as the youngest child of a large family he knew how assert himself in a crowd and fend for himself in the inevitable sibling tussles, being the sole income earner in London saw him develop administrative skills and a strong work ethic, and with his father being absent in early age, losing siblings tragically young and travelling up and down the country he knew how to thrive in the face of adversity.

Howcroft's older brother Robert had already moved to Middlesbrough where he met and married a local girl, Margaret, and opened a shop called Cooks Confectioners. James moved to the area around the same time, during the mid-1870s, where he cared for the eldest two of his brother's five children, Edith and Frederick, from his house on Queen Street, then part of the small fishing town of Coatham. He used his experience as a builder's clerk to find employment with the Kirkleatham Local Board as a surveyor, a role he would hold for five decades. Just a short walk from his house was the local YMCA, where he joined their cricket team. Here he would meet many young men who had travelled far and wide to capitalise on the economic boom that the area was experiencing thanks, in no small part, to the advancement of the steelworks. Joining Howcroft were the likes of Sep Cruse, a foundry worker from Chelsea, and Augustus Yeo, a joiner originally from Devon.

The young men at the YMCA took part in a variety of activities; from singing, arithmetic and chess to readings, recitations and bible class. It was a very common occurrence in the 1880s for such associations to also offer sporting activities, "a rational sectarian recreation to help evangelise the poor."[2] Several football teams in this period were born out of religious institutions; two-time FA Cup finalists Queen's Park came from the YMCA, Everton were founded at St. Domingo's Methodist Church and Fulham were originally called Fulham St Andrew's Church Sunday School Football Club.

Even more common were football teams formed by cricketers. Redcar and Coatham YMCA's main sporting pastime was cricket, where they came up against local clubs including a Middlesbrough team featuring Jackson Ewbank. Ewbank was a fantastic athlete, sporting a powerful moustache and a robust physique. One of the standout players in Middlesbrough's earliest football teams, the Boro captain holds the honour of being their first ever recorded goalscorer, having trials in the 1880s to play for the England national team which sadly never materialised.

Jackson Ewbank
Northern Athlete, 18th July 1883

In late 1878, the young men met to discuss how they would fill their time during the winter months when the cricket season was over. Members of the YMCA such as Augustus Yeo had spent time living in Middlesbrough, thus having an opportunity to watch first-hand what their cricket adversaries could do on a football pitch, and the time had come to see how Redcar would fare. It was decided, then, on 10th October 1878 that for outdoor exercise on a Saturday afternoon, a football club would be formed.[3]

This was the birth of Redcar and Coatham YMCA Football Club, with James Howcroft taking on the reins as secretary, his first taste of football administration but by no means the last. By 1879, they had at least 30 members and it was not long before the sport in the town became popular enough to earn column inches in the local press. One of the earliest recordings comes from what was then known as *The Daily Gazette* in March 1879, with Redcar hosting Middlesbrough. During this period there were several different sets of rules being used across the country, each with their own wildly different laws which were being amended every year. Only a few years previously, for example, it was legal for outfield players to catch the ball according to the Sheffield Rules, and the 1863 Cambridge Rules said that goals could be scored at any height provided the ball travelled between the posts. It is perhaps not too surprising, then, to learn that the 1879 game between Middlesbrough and Redcar was played in four 20-minute periods, a common - but not entirely consistent - timeframe for early football matches.

Although it was formed by cricketers, the football team initially played their home games at Redcar Racecourse, around a mile south-west of the cricket club. Perhaps there was a fear from their summer sport counterparts that the heavy-handed tactics employed by the footballers would cause too much

James Howcroft
Sports Gazette, 1st February 1919

damage to the pitch. Whatever the reason, the men would instead make their way to the Red Lion Hotel, an institution in Redcar until its demolition in 1981, to change into their black and red kits, then head south to the racecourse.

Here, in March 1879, they met a strong Middlesbrough side. Although Boro were by far the strongest team in the area, Redcar were praised in the press for their strong defensive efforts, thanks in no small part to James Howcroft's fearless command of goal. A tactic employed by forwards of this era would be to flatten the goalkeeper to make it easier to put the ball between the sticks, but Howcroft's resilient nature and powerful frame made it a tricky task, and "many a rushing enemy found the impact with his solid and stocky frame a thing to be wary of."[4] A retrospective article made a similar comment, noting that even by the turn of the century goalkeepers were given far more protection than they were in Howcroft's era, "although goalkeeping in those bygone days was far different and more dangerous than it is at the present time, like that of the policeman and the bailiff in the eyes of the law, seems to be sacred."[5] It seems that no matter how far back in time you go, you'll always find someone who thinks modern-day players are too soft compared to the hard-nosed bruisers of the past.

Despite Howcroft's bulldoggish approach to goalkeeping, the constant barrage of shots at Redcar's goal had proved too much by the end of the third 20, with Jackson Ewbank teeing up teammate Tom Dales to break the deadlock. The game was a truly mismatched affair, and although Redcar's attitude could not be called into question, the young cricketers had plenty to learn about the Beautiful Game. Some quick counter-attacking play by Augustus Yeo and Charles Baker came to nothing, with Middlesbrough's experienced defence wise to their attempts. In the last 20, WG Hildreth doubled Middlesbrough's lead and put the game out of reach.

Redcar had some growing to do, but they had talented players and a good attitude, and it would not take long for them to become a much stronger outfit. The following season, with Howcroft still as secretary, it was arranged to play their home games at the cricket club, which had the added benefit of having on-site changing facilities at the Lobster Inn, and was considered to be one of the finest grounds in the country at the time. It has changed very little in the intervening century and a half; the gables and octagonal turrets of Nelson Square and its sibling Trafalgar Terrace on the other side of the green have watched what few additions there have been to the ground, from the iron fences that were brought in from Skinningrove to the pavilion installed in the 1920s.

Their team had also improved, most significantly with the addition of the Harrison brothers who had moved to the area from Lancaster in order to further their careers as elementary school teachers. The younger brother, William, was a fine athlete with an impressive footballing brain. His mazy runs down the right flank would be talked about for decades, and his ability and tactical prowess saw him elected captain of the team.

The role of a captain in Victorian football was a far greater responsibility than the team leaders of today's game. While it was James Howcroft's job as secretary to arrange matches, secure grounds and changing facilities, acquire kits and look after finances, captains not only served as the talisman of the team, but also had the responsibility of dictating the style of football that was employed, making tactical changes during a game and had a key role in recruiting new players and selecting the starting XI.

By the time the 1879 cricket season ended and the football season began, Redcar's new recruits helped to establish "a much better team than last year,"[6] according to a *Gazette* report on their first game of the season against Loftus. William Harrison played with his brother Thomas in the forward line alongside the previous season's standout performers Charles Baker and Augustus Yeo to make a potent attacking threat. It was an "easy victory" for Redcar, with Baker netting twice and William Harrison rounding off an excellent performance with the other goal. More games were subsequently arranged throughout the season against Middlesbrough and South Bank.

Coatham Cricket Field c.1895
Royal Album of Redcar and Neighbourhood, 1895

At the time, there was a very small pool from which to draw opposition teams. South Bank were supposedly formed in 1868, but the distinct lack of suitable opponents in the club's formative years meant that very few games were actually played. With teams like Redcar, Middlesbrough and Loftus forming in the 1870s there were more opportunities to play, but most matches throughout a regular season would see those same handful of teams play against each other.

One such game was a few months later, on 29th November 1879 when they once again faced Middlesbrough. The teams trudged their way onto the field through lashings of snow which didn't relent until late into the game. After some good play from both sides in the first half in which chances were created at either end despite the horrendous conditions, Middlesbrough took the lead through Tom Dales from a corner kick. But Redcar rallied and didn't let their heads drop, William Harrison taking the game by the scruff of the neck with devastating runs down the right wing. With the game in its dying stages, Redcar carried the ball magnificently towards goal, with Augustus Yeo taking possession and astonishing the Middlesbrough support by netting the equaliser, the scores finishing level as the full-time whistle rang. Only nine months after their convincing loss to Boro, Redcar had already assembled a team that could give them a proper challenge.

Although the young club were still finding their feet, Redcar had already established a core group in a line-up that rarely changed. The team was a microcosm of the town at the time; people from Cambridgeshire, Lancashire, London and Devon were travelling to Redcar to take advantage of the increase in job opportunities and expanding middle class. Alongside workers in the nearby steelworks in the squad, there were architects, teachers and civil engineers. Howcroft, Yeo, Baker, Stickreth, Smith, Thompson, Holmes and the Harrison brothers played most of the season together, and their understanding of each other's game was beginning to pay dividends.

A little over a month later, on 17th January 1880, they once more came up against Middlesbrough, back at Redcar Racecourse. Boro were so far unbeaten in the season, and Redcar went into the game "with considerable anxiety."[7] *The Gazette* reported "a continuous attack on the home fortress" as Middlesbrough tried their best to prove that the 1-1 draw in November was a fluke, but Redcar's customary strong counter-attacking play saw Baker net himself another goal for the season. Augustus Yeo and Thomas Harrison added one more each, a 3-0 result leading the *Gazette* reporter to write:

"A surprise for the visitors that was only equalled by the astonishment and blank dismay of their defeated opponents, who, until this disastrous day, had held premier position among the associations clubs for miles around."[8]

This result was a huge milestone in the history of the club. Middlesbrough were still only a young team, having been formed four years previously, but they had already become a local powerhouse and they were forming the building blocks that would lead them all the way to the Football League in a few decades' time. To go up against the best team in the North Riding as a club barely over a year old and end their unbeaten run in such decisive fashion truly was a statement as to the ambition and rising quality of the club. These early games fanned the flames of a rivalry that saw football explode as a spectator sport in the North East over the years that followed, and invariably encouraged both teams to grow as they each chased success.

The budding rivalry was set aside the following month, though, when Middlesbrough faced the oldest club in Newcastle - Tyne Association. Redcar's second team, captained by Charles Baker, played a Middlesbrough side on the same day and were resoundingly beaten 7-0, but Boro's strongest team (minus the services of their captain Jackson Ewbank, who was representing Sheffield) travelled to Northumberland Cricket Ground. They could only muster nine players to face Tyne Association, so up stepped Redcar captain William Harrison to bring them into double figures. They wouldn't need an 11th man, as Middlesbrough won the game 1-0 thanks to a solitary William Harrison goal.

•

The Football League, the first time football teams were introduced to a season-long competition in a league format, was not formed until 1888 and teams before this point only played in friendlies - often referred to as "ordinary matches" - or cup competitions. The first time Redcar entered such a competition was the Sheffield Challenge Cup in 1880. These days it seems odd that a team from the north east coast would have thought to enter a competition based in South Yorkshire, but in the early 1880s teams in the North Riding, with no football association of their own, were actually under the auspices of the historic Sheffield Association. The Sheffield Challenge Cup – known later as the Sheffield and Hallamshire Senior Cup - was in its fifth year in 1880 and is still in place today, making it the second oldest surviving cup competition in England next to the FA Cup.

Up until 1880 it could even be argued that the Sheffield Challenge Cup was the bigger competition. The inaugural final in 1877 saw 8,000 people pack into Bramall Lane to watch The Wednesday beat Heeley 4-3, with 7,000 people watching them beat Attercliffe a year later. By comparison, the FA Cup only drew a crowd of 3,000 people to watch Wanderers beat Oxford University in 1877, and 4,500 to see them win their fifth final with a victory over Royal Engineers. 1880 was the first time the FA Cup final got a bigger attendance than the final of the Sheffield Challenge Cup; 4,000 people watched Old Carthusians dispatch Old Etonians 3-0 in the FA Cup final, while 3,000 people saw The Wednesday hand an 8-1 drubbing to Ecclesfield. Earlier in the competition, however, a modest 2,500 people came to watch Redcar's match against rivals Middlesbrough.

Middlesbrough's Linthorpe Road ground was in perfect condition for the historic encounter as the two teams prepared for another battle. William Harrison hit first for Redcar, a lead that was quickly doubled. Boro pulled a goal back before Baker "ran the gauntlet and succeeded in obtaining a third goal for Redcar." However, this was not to be a repeat of January's match, and Boro dug deep towards the end of the game and showed their superior fitness. They managed three goals without reply and forced the game to a replay.

Middlesbrough's miraculous comeback saw the replay played a week later. Unfortunately, it wasn't to be for Redcar, with Baker being made to pay for spurning some early chances before Middlesbrough went 1-0 up. Redcar did manage to equalise, but strong play from Boro's goalkeeper – one Mr Bastard, who would go on to become a referee (yes, really) – and Jackson Ewbank meant that Redcar lost 3-1. Despite the defeat, Redcar's form had skyrocketed over the course of the season, and several of their players were becoming standout performers not just in the town, but in the whole region.

One of these standouts was clearly William Harrison. Already a talented sportsman, Harrison had used the past few seasons to gain valuable experience against some top northern teams. He was tall, slim, quick and agile, with the majority of Redcar's attacking play centred on his mazy dribbles down the right. As Redcar were part of the Sheffield Association, it meant that their players were eligible to appear for their representative side who toured both England and Scotland throughout the course of the year. Middlesbrough's Jackson Ewbank had already earned that honour, and by November 1880 William Harrison had done enough to earn himself a call-up.

What a debut it was. *The Sheffield Daily Telegraph* notes that he was "the first to show prominently for his side"[9] against Birmingham, the crowd cheering his "dexterous dodging tactics, which completely nonplussed his opponents." He revelled in the opportunity to showcase his skill and eye for goal, never allowing the pressure of the occasion to affect his performance. It was clear that he was a class above his Midlands counterparts; he not only scored on his debut, but he assisted another *four* goals in an 11-2 drubbing. Harrison had arrived.

Going into the New Year, Harrison had more call-ups to juggle alongside his Redcar responsibilities. On New Year's Day 1881 he travelled with the Sheffield side to The Oval to face London, where a crowd of around 1,000 people braved the snow to watch the seventh match between the two sides. London and Sheffield first met in 1866, considered by many – including founder of the FA Cup, Charles Alcock – to be the first match of any importance to be played under the association rules. Such was the importance of these games that they were "looked upon with the same interest as we follow present day internationals,"[10] said a 1906 article. "Harrison showed up well forward for Sheffield," wrote *The Yorkshire Post*, "but the back play was not up to the mark."[11] Despite Harrison and his colleague Billy Mosforth – who would go on to make nine appearances for England – testing the London goalkeeper on numerous occasions, they were woefully outclassed and lost the game 5-0.

There was no shame in this, as London's team was a who's who of England players. Alongside occasional internationals like Harry Swepstone, Francis Sparks, Charles Wollaston and Edward Parry were some seriously heavy hitters. Norman Bailey, of reigning FA Cup champions Clapham Rovers, would go on to score 15 goals in 19 England appearances, 15 of which as captain. Clement Mitchell, goalscorer in the game against Sheffield, scored five goals in five appearances for England, and Charles Bambridge, who scored a brace in the game, managed 11 goals in 18 games during his stellar England career.

In February, Harrison and the Sheffield Association team took part in a historic occasion, travelling to Scotland to take on Glasgow at Hampden Park. Football matches between any two countries were rare at this point, and official games between England and Scotland had only been played since 1872, with this being only the fourth time that Sheffield had crossed the border to take on their Glaswegian counterparts. Their opponents were a very strong side and had an excellent record over the Yorkshiremen, this time with George Ker – who scored 10 goals in only five matches for Scotland – and Eadie Fraser – another Scotland international – contributing to a 3-0 win. Not the results Sheffield wanted, but Harrison was impressing in both England and Scotland against some of the best players in the game.

Sheffield Association side, 1881. William Harrison is on the front row on the left, sat on the floor.[1]
Green 'un, 23rd November 1922

•

Harrison may have been turning heads around the country but back in the North East, all was not well. *The York Herald* reported "disorganisation induced by the severe weather of the past few weeks," with fixtures "mixed in a very topsey-turvy fashion."[12] The teams needed help in making sure that their fixtures could be played out, and they needed a place to air their grievances to make sure that misdemeanours – the more creative examples being swearing referees and people lying about their ages – were punished accordingly. This led to the first general meeting of the newly-

---

[1] Back row (left to right): GB Marples (Staveley), TE Crawley (Wednesday), J Gregory (Ecclesfield), JR Harvey (hon. secretary), A Woodcock (Holmes).
Middle row: WF Beardshaw (Attercliffe), T Buttery (Exchange), W Pierce-Dix (umpire), J Hunter (Heeley), TH Fletcher (Pyebank), W Mosforth (Wednesday)
Front row: W Harrison (Redcar), R Gregory (Wednesday).

formed Cleveland Football Association in February 1881 at the Swatters Carr in Middlesbrough.

With its formation came greater organisation of the game in the region including fully-established rules, a commitment to form clubs in areas that were not yet represented, a county XI to play other representative sides in the country and a new cup competition – the imaginatively-named Cleveland Challenge Cup, which is currently known as the North Riding Senior Cup. It also meant that Cleveland had a chair at the Football Association conferences alongside representatives from all over the UK.

Cleveland FA advert, 1883
Northern Athlete, 12th September 1883

The *Yorkshire Post* reported that by March 1881 the Cleveland FA had 400 members across 11 clubs, and they were hoping to "raise a challenge cup worthy of the association, and one of the value of £100 is expected to be procured."[13] In today's money, that's £12,250. The *York Herald* described the cup as "a beautiful example of the silversmith's art," with engravings "to give local significance, a group of blast furnaces, with pig beds, engines, trucks etc."[14]

The competition officially began in the 1881/82 season and Redcar, off the back of results like a 3-2 victory over Middlesbrough, a 9-3 demolition of Marske and a resounding 7-0 win against Whitby, were unsurprisingly projected to do well. "We must congratulate the Redcar captain on the good team he has got together, and the team on their evident good practice,"[15] wrote *The York Herald*. The semi-final was a double-header, with 1,000 people travelling to Middlesbrough to watch Redcar take on Whitby and Middlesbrough play North Ormesby. Boro comfortably won 7-1, but the *Newcastle Journal* reported that Redcar's game was "the most exciting that has taken place for the cup trophy,"[16] with Harrison scoring "the best goal we have seen got,"[17] according to *The York Herald*, winning 2-1 and securing Redcar's place in the final against Middlesbrough.

That meant that Boro and Redcar, now firmly established as rivals for superiority of the North Riding, met in the final in front of 1,500 people, including the "gentry of the district."[18] Glorious weather met the two teams as they made their way out to the field in Middlesbrough for the first ever Cleveland Challenge Cup final. They both exchanged attacks at the start of the game, before William Harrison picked up the ball from a corner and smashed it in off the crossbar. Advantage Redcar. Boro pressed the Redcar goal yet again, but they were equal to their attacks, and soon the ball was back into Boro's territory. "The Middlesbro' goal was fraught with evil," said *The York Herald*, with Ransford scoring an own goal which doubled Redcar's advantage. James Howcroft in the Redcar goal was resilient, and bravely fought off the oncoming attacks from the Middlesbrough men. Then shortly before half-time, "the final result looked to be a certain victory for the visitors" as Shepherd put Redcar 3-0 up.

But football is a game of two halves. The prevailing wind which had assisted Redcar in the first half was now behind Middlesbrough, and captain Jackson Ewbank made some tactical changes to the Boro line-up. Despite Howcroft being praised for "parrying attack after attack," Redcar couldn't hold on forever. After the Redcar goalkeeper pushed away a shot from Albert Borrie, Thompson arrived to tap it in. Game on. Continuing their attack, Cochrane was scythed down by Abbey, with Pickstock scoring the free-kick and making it 3-2. "The excitement was now intense," wrote *The York Herald*, with both sides giving it everything. Then, just five minutes from time, "amid uproarious cheering"[19] Middlesbrough equalised. For a second time in as many years, Middlesbrough had clawed back a draw after going 3-0 down against Redcar.

The replay was an "absorbing topic of conversation" for the week leading up to the match, and "every scrap of news relating to the training and composition of the respective teams was eagerly seized upon and discussed." Redcar had improved their team considerably since the last game, with Addison Fiddler being moved to his usual place as full back instead of the forward position he had found himself in a fortnight previously, with Marson travelling from Grantham and Oxford native Wethey also taking up arms for their old team.

Howcroft once again excelled when the match got underway, "deservedly gaining the heartiest applause from the partisans of both clubs,"[20] and it looked like Redcar would make up for throwing away their three goal advantage in the first match after scoring first. Boro equalised in the second half, and a "severe struggle ensued,"[21] leading into the final minutes. Boro pressed, and Redcar defended for their lives, until at the death Middlesbrough once again broke Redcar hearts and scored the winner. "This success was received with tremendous cheering, waving of handkerchiefs, and tossing of hats," said *The York Herald*. Prizes were then presented to the Middlesbrough team, becoming the first holders of the trophy. It would not be their last.

Naturally disappointed, especially considering his fine individual performance, James Howcroft still had a lot to celebrate in 1882. On 13th December at St Peter's Church in Redcar, Howcroft married Rose Ann Hoggard, the daughter of renowned photographer Samuel Hoggard whose cartes de visite are still in circulation today. The couple would have one daughter, Violet, who in keeping with the family's sporting tradition would go on to marry a well-known Redcar cricketer. But Howcroft's greatest sporting achievements were still ahead of him.

Chapter 2: Competition

The Cleveland representative side, benefitting from the rapid growth of teams in the area, were becoming a force to be reckoned with in the early 1880s. The Cleveland Football Association was officially formed in February 1881, and they immediately set about organising their first game. Northumberland and Durham, another new association, visited Middlesbrough Cricket Field amid torrid rain for the historic occasion. Cleveland's opponents drew most of their players from Sunderland, Haughton and Tyne Association. For Cleveland, with the exception of one Whitby player, everyone came from either Redcar or Middlesbrough. Alongside Redcar's James Howcroft, Addison Fidler and Sep Cruse came a forward partnership of devastating proportions. The two most skilful players in the North East, William Harrison and Jackson Ewbank, would finally compete side-by-side. A later article would reminisce, "Ewbank was one of the finest dribblers of his time, he and Bill Harrison, of Redcar, with his corkscrew dribbles, being a pair of champions."[22] Their partnership proved to be a deadly combination, with both men getting on the scoresheet in an emphatic 10-0 victory.

Cleveland had proved they had the quality to overcome another young association side, but how would they fare against a more experienced one? A few months later they played against an Edinburgh team made up mainly of Hearts and Hibs players, this coming only nine years after the first ever official international match between the same two nations. *The York Herald* described the game, played on Christmas Eve, as "the most important match ever fixed to be played in Middlesbrough," with Edinburgh choosing "some of the best players in Scotland."[23] Cleveland narrowly lost the game 3-2. Messrs Bradbury and Cruse were Redcar's representatives in the game, while Jackson Ewbank captained the squad, although William Harrison also had the honour of captaining the Cleveland side on many occasions.

Speaking of Harrison, he was having a productive few years himself. Between 1881 and 1882 he would continue to represent Sheffield, appearing no fewer than 14 times in matches that would be reported in newspapers as far away as India. He played alongside a host of England internationals against some of the best representative sides the country had to offer. He was deemed one of the best players on the pitch by the *Sheffield Independent* in their match against Lancashire - scoring in the reverse fixture - and assisted a goal in a historic win against Glasgow, the first time Sheffield had managed to beat them in nine attempts. He was "half paralysed"[24] in a game against Berks and Bucks, receiving a "rare outburst of applause"[25] after bravely coming back on 15 minutes later.

He also inspired Sheffield to a 3-2 victory over the North of England, playing against Middlesbrough duo Pickstock and Cochrane, as well as Redcar compatriot Tom

Bradbury. The game was arranged to determine who would represent the North in the prestigious North vs South game at the Oval later in the season.

Sheffield Association side that defeated Glasgow in 1882. William Harrison is on the middle row, second from the left.[2]
Courtesy of Sheffield Wednesday Football Club

The North vs South matches acted as international trials to decide the England team, and William Harrison's impressive performances had earned him the privilege of playing for his right to wear the three lions. To say these games featured legends is an understatement. Charles Bambridge played for The South, who captained England and was their top scorer for three years, as did another England captain – Norman Bailey. There was a host of FA Cup winners on either side, and even the match officials were legendary; with Sir Francis Marindin, who became president of the FA, and CW Alcock, founder of the FA Cup, officiating the game.

---

[2] Back row (left to right): JC Shaw (president), JR Harvey (hon. secretary), H Wilkinson (Wednesday), WE Clegg (vice president), J Stevens (Pyebank), JC Clegg (umpire), E Buttery (Wednesday), WP Dix (referee).
Middle row: J Hudson (Wednesday), W Harrison (Redcar), J Hunter (Heeley), TE Cowley (Burton Star), W Mosforth (Wednesday)
Front row: H Winterbottom (Heeley), A Mallinson (Barnsley), HP Marple (Staveley).

So many Northerners refused the call down to London that they had to play with a Southerner – RA Lunnon, captain of Buckinghamshire's Great Marlow. Lunnon was already known to Harrison and many of his northern compatriots, which exemplifies the incestuousness of early first-class football and the tiny world in which its occupants lived. Harrison's Sheffield side had come up against Lunnon's Berks and Bucks in 1881, which featured a prominent member of the southern side; Arthur Bambridge, brother of Charles who had made his debut for England the previous year.

Sadly, despite the *Nottingham Evening Post* writing that his performances for the North deserved "special mention,"[26] Harrison was not selected to represent his country. He had to compete against England legend Charles Bambridge for the outside right position, which was no easy feat. England went on to win their game against Ireland 13-0. There was an experimental law at the time whereby a referee could award a goal if he deemed one had been prevented by a deliberate handball, but it is unknown whether this law was utilised in the game. Although he would never wear the three lions, many of Harrison's most memorable achievements were still to come.

•

Despite Redcar's Cleveland Cup final loss to Middlesbrough, by the end of 1882 they were well and truly established as a major force across all of northern England, meeting allegedly the world's oldest workplace team Lockwood Brothers at Bramall Lane in Sheffield (which was hosting full international football matches at this time) in front of a "large company of spectators"[27] against a team featuring Harrison's Sheffield compatriot Winterbottom. Despite a disallowed goal for Redcar, they ended up drawing the game 3-3.

Although Harrison had suffered disappointment when it came to international selection, he had something else on his checklist: Competing in the FA Cup. In the later stages of the 1882/83 competition, a famous team would ask for Harrison's services. Without some key players, Sheffield Wednesday enlisted the help of Harrison alongside Pyebank's Betts and Bentley of Walkley for their third round tie against Forest. Being called into action by Wednesday was a huge honour at this point in time; the previous season they had reached the semi-finals, losing to Blackburn Rovers in a replay after a goalless draw.

When Wednesday came up against Nottingham Forest, Harrison scored in a 2-2 draw, then scored twice and assisted the other in the 3-2 win in the replay. His name also appeared in a *Sporting Life* article in February detailing a list of probable teams for the fourth round tie against Notts County, but he did not feature. "The Wednesday team were much weakened by the absence of Harrison, of Redcar, whose place was taken by Bowns,"[28] wrote *The Nottingham Evening Post* of the game. Without his game-changing attacking play, Wednesday lost the game and were unable to reach the heights of the previous season.

As was fairly common practice at the time, Forest has decided to lodge a complaint against the three new faces in the Wednesday team, claiming they were not eligible. With Redcar still technically being part of the Sheffield FA despite the formation of the Cleveland FA, and players still allowed to represent more than one club at a time, the case was dismissed. "This is very midsummer madness," wrote *The Sheffield Daily Telegraph*, "Harrison, as one of the best players in the clubs within the Sheffield Association, has been played for Sheffield."[29]

Harrison was also busy juggling his Redcar and Sheffield obligations, travelling up and down the county to play two legs of the famous Glasgow vs Sheffield match at the same time. Incidentally, the Sheffield Association also played a match against the Cleveland side in February, but Harrison's potential dilemma on who to represent was resolved by the announcement that the members of Sheffield's first XI that took on Glasgow were barred from playing. Tom Alvey and Tom Bradbury were partnered at the back alongside Sep Cruse, all Redcar men, but they could not prevent the Sheffield onslaught that saw them come away 5-0 winners.

A Redcar Baines card
Courtesy of the National Football Museum

By the 1883/84 season Redcar finally entered a team into the FA Cup, the only representatives of the North East alongside Middlesbrough, who were also in their first season in the competition. By a strange quirk of fate, they were also drawn against Nottingham Forest, who would be semi-finalists the following season and would go on to win the competition just over a decade later. Although Harrison had shown precisely what he could do against them, he wouldn't get a chance to repeat the previous season's efforts. There are some conflicting reports about what exactly happened, as most newspapers simply stated that Redcar telegraphed the day before the match to say that they were unable to get a team together. The *Athletic News* reported, however, that Redcar - the away team - wanted Forest to pay their expenses, and forfeited the match when they refused to do so.

Whatever the real reason was, Redcar did not compete in the FA Cup in 1883, but they still had plenty to be positive about. Coming up against the experienced South

Bank, one of the oldest clubs in the region, in the Cleveland Challenge Cup semi-final earlier in the year you would have been forgiven for thinking it would have been a close encounter. Redcar scored *nine* goals without reply, including a hat-trick from William Harrison who scored his first goal by taking the ball the full length of the field. James Howcroft had so little work to do in the Redcar goal that he was "sitting on the boundary rope most of the time talking to his friends."[30]

The win put them through to their second Cleveland Challenge Cup final, and they once again faced Middlesbrough. Scores of people from all over the area packed the trains to Darlington where the final was held. Despite the freezing conditions, the attendance was "larger than at any match for a long time past."[31] The match was held in two 40-minute periods, and Middlesbrough were so dominant in the first 40 that, despite losing two men to injury, they crossed the boundary ropes at half-time finding themselves 2-0 up.

William Harrison halved the deficit in the second 40, but the nine men of Middlesbrough restored their two goal cushion. Another Redcar goal set up a tense finish, and this was their chance to make amends for twice snatching a draw from the jaws of victory in two 3-3 matches against Boro, but the equaliser never came. Middlesbrough retained the trophy and Redcar's hunt for silverware continued.

•

In October 1883, a matter of months after William Harrison inspired Sheffield Wednesday to victory in the FA Cup, he would bring his Redcar team to Bramall Lane to play against them in the Sheffield Challenge Cup. *The Sheffield and Rotherham Independent* described the match as a meeting of two "first-rate clubs,"[32] but despite sending a strong team across to South Yorkshire, Wednesday were just too good for them. Redcar tried their best to bring the game to Wednesday, but the match finished 7-1. Several Sheffield-based publications were nevertheless full of praise for the Redcar side. *The Sheffield Telegraph* noted Harrison's previous work for their Association side, saying that not only did he come close to scoring but "once he worked the ball so admirably that one of his colleagues was able to get it past George Ulyett in goal."[33] Ulyett was a seasoned sportsman and had already represented England in a first-class cricket career that lasted 20 years.

Despite disappointment against arguably one of the strongest teams in the country, Redcar had plenty to celebrate in October 1883. When they sent a team to face Middlesbrough without the help of at least three key players, one of them being William Harrison who was on Sheffield duty, it was said that some spectators were offering odds of 10/1 against Redcar. When the first goal was scored by Redcar, the faintest of cheers were heard from the crowd compared to the uproarious applause when Boro scored the equaliser. So when Redcar went back in front, "one was almost moved to laugher on looking round and seeing the horror-stricken countenances of the home team supporters." The match ended 2-1 to Redcar in an excellent performance from a far from full-strength team, with one Middlesbrough player who had travelled from Edinburgh especially for the game left to think about some of his life choices. "Poor fellow, his heart must be sad, like the hearts of some of his comrades," wrote The North Eastern Weekly Gazette, "for I am informed they have not been seen to smile since Saturday."[34]

Although Redcar did not compete in the 1883/84 FA Cup, just by being in the hat they found themselves at the forefront of the biggest change in modern football. In fact, this was arguably the beginning of modern football. Up until the 1880/81 season, every previous FA Cup finalist was a team made up of public school Old Boys, with only six different teams in 10 years; Wanderers, Royal Engineers, Oxford University, Old Etonians, Clapham Rovers and Old Carthusians. 1881/82 was the first time a northern working class team made it to the final, with Blackburn Rovers losing 1-0 to Old Etonians, the following year seeing Blackburn Olympic finally bringing the trophy north when they defeated Old Etonians after extra time.

The season that Redcar scratched to Nottingham Forest was the first time that an elite southern team failed to make it to the final, and they never would again. The 1883/84 season ended with Blackburn Rovers winning 2-1 over Scotland's Queen's Park. This was the beginning of the competition we know today, and represented the significant power shift from the Old Boys who had dominated the sport for decades to the northern powerhouses that brought the game to the working classes.

From here on, although Harrison did still occasionally appear for Redcar, as well as the Cleveland and Sheffield representative sides, they were fewer and farther between. He was offered a job as an assistant school inspector in Kent, furthering the career in education that had originally brought him to Redcar. Professionalism in football was banned until 1885, so there are many cases during this period where talented players suddenly stop playing in order to focus on their careers, no longer being able to justify the commitment of playing football all around the country alongside a full-time job and family life. "He will probably forswear football now,"[35] wrote The Athletic News.

Not quite. Just a matter of weeks later, Harrison guested for FA Cup holders Blackburn Olympic for a local match-up against Blackburn Park Road. Despite appearing for the team that had proven themselves as the best club in the land by wrestling the FA Cup from the hands of Old Etonians, it took a matter of minutes for Harrison to make his mark. Playing uphill and against the wind in the first half, he scored the first goal in a 4-1 win.

Even being down in Kent didn't diminish his involvement in the game. His proximity to the capital meant that he was available to be an umpire at a London Challenge Cup game between holders Upton Park, who won Gold at the 1900 Olympics representing

Great Britain, and Tottenham Hotspur. Upton Park had Charles Bambridge in their line-up, who Harrison had tried, unsuccessfully, to oust from his England position a few years previously. He still made the effort to travel for occasional appearances in some of the higher-profile matches in the North East, including one last appearance for Cleveland against Scarborough, where he would play alongside future Redcar goalkeeper Dawkings.

Dawkings smoking his pipe
Northern Review, 17th March 1888

Dawkings, a goalkeeper who was never seen without a pipe in his mouth (even between the sticks), was still a Middlesbrough player in 1884, and came up against Harrison in the third Cleveland Challenge Cup final between the two teams. This was to be the biggest meeting between the two yet, as almost 4,000 people packed into the Coatham Cricket Ground, and despite *The York Herald* noting a "hard struggle throughout for supremacy,"[36] Redcar were faced with injury problems before the game even started. Forced to make a change to replace Simpson, one of their best forwards, the only available replacement was also injured and only lasted five minutes. With Redcar playing almost the entirety of the game with 10 men, Middlesbrough once again came away with the victory with the game ending 3-0.

Although it was another disappointing result, Harrison was present at the club's annual meeting two weeks later, and with good reason. After six years of service to the club which saw them elevated from an inexperienced team from a tiny seaside town to one of the strongest clubs in the North of England, Harrison was officially recognised for his efforts. "The chief event of the evening was the presentation of a handsome gold watch to Mr Harrison, who has so long and ably acted as captain to the club," said the report in the *Gazette*, "and an exceedingly pleasant evening was spent."[37]

Then came his last hurrah in South Yorkshire. As Christmas approached, William took the trek north to spend the festive period with his family. Unmarried with no children, his journey took him not to Redcar or his hometown of Lancaster, but Sheffield, where his older brother and former Redcar player Thomas was living. Interestingly, he was living at the top of Abbeydale Road, not half a mile from Bramall Lane. And as fate would have it, his visit to Sheffield not only coincided with a Sheffield Wednesday game (who were the tenants of Bramall Lane at that time), but many of his old colleagues were unable to play the match against FA Cup holders Blackburn Rovers (a fixture that would be repeated only a couple of years later in the FA Cup final in front of a crowd of 20,000) and they needed players.

A very popular figure in South Yorkshire, the crowd were delighted to see that he had been convinced to don the famous blue and white stripes once again. But he was well and truly out of practice and Blackburn, inspired by the likes of Fergus Suter, made famous to modern fans as the star of Netflix's *The English Game*, had already proved themselves to be the best team in the country after their FA Cup victory. Harrison was "rushing into football from the enervating toil of school inspectorship,"[38] wrote one newspaper, "though everyone was glad to see him on the field." Despite holding their own in a 1-1 draw, and some occasional dazzling runs that had made him a hit in Sheffield, it was not the perfect swansong. The *Sheffield Daily Telegraph* nicely sums up the high regard in which he was held, and the disappointment of his performance:

"One pleasant feature was the reappearance on the field of Mr. Harrison, late of Redcar, who is on a visit to Sheffield, and he was prevailed upon to take his place among his old compatriots. Mr. Harrison, however, was evidently out of practice, and before he again leaves for the South we hope to see him when he has re-acquired his unrivalled dodging tactics and general good play."

They would not have to wait long to see it. Blackburn Olympic, FA Cup winners for whom he had guested at the start of the year, had a return match against Sheffield Wednesday to play after dismantling them 12-0 earlier in the season. Wednesday needed quality to save themselves from another embarrassing scoreline, and this time Harrison would not disappoint. Olympic had seen first hand what Harrison could do, and this time he notched up a superb assist in an impressive 6-0 win on Boxing Day.

This was his last ever game in Sheffield. No longer playing regular football, his days in the Sheffield Association side were long gone, and his three goals and one assist in two competitive Sheffield Wednesday games left a legacy that thrilled fans at the time and confused present day historians. "A total unknown in the annals of Wednesday's history,"[39] wrote one such modern publication.

Harrison's time in Sheffield may have been over and his Redcar appearances may have been sporadic, but he had plenty more to offer. 1884/85 was a historic season for the club because they would finally compete in the FA Cup. It was a big one, too, because they had been drawn against Sunderland, and the virtue of a home tie meant no funny business with expenses. Although the young Redcar team started well and quickly went 3-0 up, Sunderland came back into the game in the second half and scored within five minutes of the restart, and "looked as if they would win" according to a fairly optimistic *Sunderland Daily Echo* report. Despite a second Sunderland goal being ruled out for offside, the score remained 3-1, Sunderland didn't win and Redcar progressed to the next round.

Despite the impressive victory, something even more special happened in this game, because there is evidence to suggest that this match featured one of the first ever recorded examples of a goal scored by an overhead kick. Many South American countries lay claim to the honour, some more dubious than others, after the sport popularised by English seafarers via the docks. One of the more widely accepted claims is from 1914, courtesy of a Chilean named Ramon Unzaga, but that man William Harrison got there much earlier. *The York Herald* reported that Redcar's second goal came about when "Harrison kicked the ball over his head," which was "loudly applauded."[40] *The Sunderland Echo* said the same, "a magnificent shot over his head, cheer after cheer greeting the feat."[41] It would be decades until a universal term for the move was coined; nevertheless, from what we know about William Harrison's creative attacking play, a deliberate attempt at goal by kicking the ball over his head can only conjure up one image: An overhead kick.

Upwards of 3,000 people descended upon Grimsby as they hosted Redcar in "one of the ties of the second round,"[42] so said the *Lincolnshire Chronicle*. "Redcar beat Grimsby by three goals to one." reported *The Field (The Country Gentlemen's Newspaper)*[43], which unfortunately was not the case. *The York Herald* had a more accurate report, noting that Redcar scored the first goal, although Grimsby equalised before half-time. With the wind at their backs, which was of huge tactical benefit in those days, Grimsby had the ascendancy in the second half and came away 3-1 winners. It wasn't the ideal start for their first FA Cup campaign, but they did lose to a team who, upon their second FA Cup semi-final appearance a few decades later, would set the record attendance at Old Trafford, which still stands today.

Despite some noteworthy performances in their first foray into the English Cup, there were some insidious rumblings that would continue to affect the club for the rest of their existence. During this period, Redcar had played some "ordinary matches" against Loftus, which they lost. This was nothing to be ashamed of, the teams had been playing each other since the 1870s and the two often put each other to the sword. However, for one reason or another, the Redcar fans were not happy about their most recent defeat. "It was with difficulty that the Loftus team got off the field," said *The North Eastern Weekly Gazette*. "They were hustled about with considerable violence, and the youngest of the team – Ted Rowland – was knocked down, and brutally kicked."[44] Understandably, this behaviour drew considerable criticism. "When a man loses his coin on a horse race, he does not 'go' for the jockey who wins, neither does he kick the winning horse," the article concluded.

Tom Alvey
Northern Review, 1st January 1887

It didn't end there. Outraged by these accusations, future Redcar captain Tom Alvey penned a reply. In it, he argued that Loftus gave as good as they got, who he said "made themselves generally obnoxious." He suggested that the incident with young Ted Rowland being kicked had been confused with an on-field incident in which he was accidentally hit, but nevertheless the remarks were "untrue, and likely to affect the prestige of the Redcar Club."[45] The author of the original article stated that he saw nothing that he should retract, and stood by his initial statements despite Alvey's claims to the contrary. Over the coming years, the subject of Redcar's prestige would continue to take the limelight as more instances of internal dissonance came to light.

Chapter 3: Forces Divided

By 1885, there were improvements in Redcar that propelled it from a simple Victorian fishing town into a modern-day seaside resort. The town's Board of Health was formed and was responsible for drainage, gas lighting and water quality. An extensive reservoir was built, with a new water pipe system installed to provide the people of Redcar - although, controversially, not Coatham - cheap water from a nearby spring. It had become a pleasant place to live, and as the town grew, so too did its football teams.

Alongside the improvements to the area came a new club, who would go on to become the longest-running team in the town's history: Redcar Crusaders. Playing in striking black and white halved jerseys, the first mention of the Crusaders is in 1884/85, competing in the Cleveland Junior Challenge Cup. They didn't just compete that season, they actually won the competition at their first attempt, knocking out the likes of South Bank Excelsior, Linthorpe and, as fate would have it, Redcar and Coatham to reach the final against Grove Hill Juniors.

Crusaders didn't have to travel far, the final being played at Coatham Cricket Ground on a glorious spring afternoon. George McCrie, a promising young back, led the Crusaders onto the field in front thousands of spectators, eagerly lining up to watch future stars do battle. "It was not difficult to see after the first five minutes which was the better team"[46] said one report, with Lapsley opening the scoring for Redcar after drilling the ball straight over the Grove Hill keeper's head. Sexton scored a second for Redcar after half-time, Pearson put the result beyond doubt after "rushing the ball through against all opposition,"[47] with Patton putting the icing on the cake after a neatly-taken fourth.

In winning the game, *The Northern Echo* said that Crusaders "showed the stamp of masters,"[48] a hearty three cheers ringing out from around the ground at the final whistle. The team were later entertained at the residence of their chairman Alexander Holmes, a grocer who was apparently something of an expert in the world of cheese. But despite the young team's deserved victory, they would not take home any medals, instead receiving travelling bags for their efforts.

In fairness, they did still win a trophy. *The Gazette* described it as a "handsome cup," stating it "is solid silver, is of chaste design, standing 13 inches in height, and is mounted on an ebony pedestal. On one side is a bas-relief showing the game being played."[49] Its initial value was over £800 in today's money, with more value added in the shape of a silver cover which was included later.

Crusaders may have knocked Redcar and Coatham out of the Cleveland Junior Cup, but the town's original team were still a force to be reckoned with in the senior competition. The 1884/85 season saw them reach their fourth Cleveland Challenge Cup final in a row, and for the fourth time they were up against Middlesbrough. Some misfortune had hit Redcar in previous finals; not least some very late comebacks, injuries and absent players. Unfortunately, this year would be no different. "Some people thought that Redcar had a much better chance this year of beating Middlesbrough," wrote *The North Eastern Weekly Gazette*, "but, unfortunately for the Redcar Club, three of their best players were suffering from illness."[50]

The Cleveland Junior Cup trophy

Arriving at the Cricket Ground in Darlington for the game, it was clear that William Harrison, unfortunately, was one of them. He had been living in Kent for almost two years by then, but still travelled to assist Redcar when his time allowed. "Harrison, their captain, did not exhibit that dash which usually characterises his play," the article continued. Without his pace and skill, Redcar were simply rudderless. "Stop Harrison's little game, and you nonplus the whole team,"[51] an earlier article once posited. John Bulman, who would become Redcar's secretary at the end of the season, found it impossible to keep up with Middlesbrough's attacking force of Borrie, Thompson and Pringle. Bob Agar, too, despite playing an excellent game, should not have been on the pitch. "In fact, so ill was he that when he arrived on the field he was unable to don his jersey, which had to be put on him."

Despite a valiant effort on the part of Redcar's ailing defenders, a 3-0 loss followed, with Middlesbrough's goalkeeper Dawkings allegedly only touching the ball twice throughout the whole game. As Dawkings and co. collected their gold medals, though, Redcar finally had something for their efforts. For the first time in four years, the losing team were presented with silver medals, a deserved prize for their battles with Middlesbrough over the years.

But the disappointment of another Cleveland Cup final defeat would soon dissipate, and with good reason, because Redcar were determined to improve on their FA Cup form from the previous season. Their campaign started in October 1885, with Sunderland returning to Teesside for a rematch of last season's cup opener. There was to be no revenge from the Wearsiders, however, as Redcar came away with a convincing 3-0 win. Among the scorers were George Hikeley, who was a promising youth product, and AC Tofts, a master at Coatham Grammar School who had signed from Darlington.

The win set up a tie with Lincoln Lindum a month later, who Redcar comfortably beat 2-0 in a fast-paced game in which they also had a third disallowed. It was said that the crowd was so poor that Lincoln had barely anything to show for their travels to the North East. Nevertheless, Redcar had progressed to the next round, with their fortunes increasing when they received byes for the next two rounds. In those days, fixtures were split into regional 'divisions', with Redcar falling into the Northern Sixth Division. Owing to their would-be opponents being disqualified for both the third and fourth rounds, Redcar progressed straight to the fifth round. They weren't the only ones, as the fourth round only featured two matches, every other team either being disqualified or receiving byes.

Arthur Charles Tofts
Centre for Local Studies at Darlington Library

Their next encounter was to be one of the biggest matches of the season, because they were drawn against some old foes. It was an opportunity to atone for all of the past defeats, the Cleveland Challenge Cup finals disappointments, the Sheffield Challenge Cup losses, the heartache of so often being second best. Here was a game to put it all right. The FA Cup fifth round was Redcar vs Middlesbrough.

Unsurprisingly, thousands of people travelled to Coatham Cricket Ground to watch the match, braving the January snow which threatened to jeopardise the game. But despite the wretched[52] weather, it went ahead. Redcar started brightly and drew first blood, but Boro pegged them back to go into half-time level. "In the second half the blinding snow came down fast, but did not at all stop the play," wrote *The Northern Echo*. Redcar turned up the heat (not literally obviously. See; snow) and went 2-1 up. They scored another, which was disallowed, but Boro couldn't find a way back into the game. So many times before had Redcar taken the lead against Middlesbrough, only to suffer heartbreak in the dying stages, but this time they learned from their past experiences and held firm. The final whistle rang, marking what is arguably the town's greatest ever footballing achievement. For the first time in their history, and the only time since, Redcar reached the quarter-finals of the FA Cup.

Their opponents in the last eight were Small Heath Alliance, who are better known today as Birmingham City. If *Athletic News'* colourful report is anything to go by, Small Heath were not favourites:

"Anyone prophesysing [sic] that the Alliance would see the semi-final of this classic contest at the commencement of the season would have been classed as an idiot, or perhaps a lunatic suffering with Small Heath mania, or some other delirious complaint, and the great probability is that his friends would have taken immediate steps for his future safe custody."[53]

Muntz Street, home to Small Heath Alliance

This was to be Redcar's first away match in their cup run as 6,000 people piled into Muntz Street - known at the time as Coventry Road - despite the counter-attraction of another quarter-final being played down the road at West Brom. Upon joining the Football Alliance League in 1889, it would take Small Heath another four years to attract a crowd that matched the one that came to watch them take on Redcar, such was the excitement surrounding the game. "Scarcely, if ever in the annals of the Alliance career has the Coventry Road enclosure presented a more animated appearance,"[54] wrote one publication.

Small Heath kicked off, "but fell rapidly away,"[55] allowing the Redcar forwards to make the devastating runs that had spelt the demise of so many top clubs in the North. They felt the loss of William Harrison, unable to play due to work commitments in Kent, and found themselves ineffectual down the right side, but former Middlesbrough player Charles Pauls presented a greater danger with his lightning quick runs down the left flank.

After about quarter of an hour the home team began to get a stranglehold on the game, the scores staying level only thanks to the heroics of James Howcroft in goal and Tom Alvey in front of him. 30 minutes in, though, and Redcar were made to pay for not capitalising on their early dominance when Davenport fizzed in a shot from the right hand side which flew through the sticks "amidst a score of indescribable enthusiasm around the ropes," giving Small Heath the advantage.

The score remained the same at the change of ends, with a barrage of shots from both sides when the teams resumed for the second period. Heroics at either end prevented any more goals, with Hedges and Evetts - Small Heath's answer to Howcroft and Alvey - somehow managing to prevent an equaliser. Despite their chances to level the game, though, Redcar were powerless to stop Thomas Davenport scoring his sixth goal of the campaign to make it 2-0. Their advantage could have been increased late in the game, but "Howcroft kept goal in first-class style."

The game finished 2-0, with the Alliance deservedly progressing to the semi-finals. Redcar had shown a good account of themselves, but the long trip to the West Midlands, the raucous crowd of 6,000 passionately cheering for their opponents and the William Harrison-sized hole on the right wing meant that the odds were stacked against them, nevertheless they had made history. Not only that, but they had made a name for themselves at a national level. "Small Heath has attained this very object, not by chance, but by the aid of their own exertions," the colourful *Athletic News* article concluded, "for have they not defeated such powerful combinations as Darwen, of old renown; Derby County, vanquishers of Aston Villa; Davenham, the pride and hope of Cheshire; and lastly, Redcar, the famous Yorkshiremen." That would make a good name for a book...

•

Edward Pauls
Courtesy of Edzard Pauls

Owing to his commitments as a school inspector, William Harrison had not been present during Redcar's historic cup run, the captaincy instead falling to Tom Bradbury. But he was not the only player to see his appearances limited due to his career in education. Charles Pauls, who had joined the club alongside his brother Edward after appearing for both Linthorpe and Middlesbrough, had started on his own journey to become a schoolmaster. Obtaining a first class degree in chemistry from the University of Cambridge, he studied for his Masters at Manchester, but he continued his footballing career whilst studying in Lancashire. Initially playing for Dalton Hall, the university's football team, he also represented Manchester when the two clubs amalgamated. His experience in

Teesside had served him well for the footballing challenges ahead, and "he was generally looked upon as the class of man much above the matches he used to take part in."[56]

By the end of the 1880s he was living in Preston, having found work first as a science master at Claremont College in Blackpool and later as senior assistant master at a grammar school nearby, and he attracted interest from a local team that was much more suited to his talents. Preston North End, FA Cup holders known as the original "Invincibles" after they won the Football League and the FA Cup in 1888/89 without losing a game, were impressed by Pauls' blistering speed and dazzling runs and offered him a trial in early 1890. He scored in a 10-1 win over Witton in a friendly, which was enough to convince the committee to select him for a competitive match: another FA Cup quarter-final.

A crowd of 12,000 packed into Deepdale to watch the holders take on Bolton Wanderers, and the fans were full of expectation. Sadly, despite strong attacking play from North End which saw them come from behind in the first

Charles Pauls
Courtesy of Edzard Pauls

half after going a goal down, Bolton rallied late in the game and managed to snatch a late winner, and so Pauls, despite two bites at the cherry, never managed to reach an FA Cup semi-final.

He played several more notable friendlies against Corinthian, Vale of Leven, Battlefield, Bolton and a South of England select side, but his most memorable contributions came in three competitive appearances on the way to winning the Football League title yet again for the Lilywhites. Just four years after making history with Redcar, Pauls had found himself at the very top of the footballing world.

Also briefly appearing for nearby Halliwell, he came back to Teesside long enough to contribute to Ironopolis' victorious Northern League campaign in 1891. By 1893, though, he had moved to Devon to take a role as a science master where he also trained their football team. Fourteen years at Rutlish School in Merton followed, and he spent the remainder of his years in Wales. An impressive career, both in his profession and in football, Charles Pauls was a shining example of the talent that the North East could produce and proved that the leap from playing for a Redcar side to a team at the very highest level was not quite as far as many would think. He was one of the first to do it, but many would follow in his footsteps.

•

Back to 1886 and in the wake of Small Heath mania, Redcar had achieved something that was unimaginable just a few years previously. Not only were Crusaders bringing silverware to the town having only just been formed, Redcar's more established side were counting themselves amongst the likes of Birmingham City, West Brom and Blackburn Rovers in the quarter-finals of the country's most prestigious tournament and nurturing talent that could be counted amongst the best in the world.

This was to be a period of transition, though. Redcar and Coatham would never again reach the highs of the 1885/86 season, exemplified by their loss in the Cleveland Cup final replay a few months later. Despite once again coming up against Middlesbrough, with their FA Cup achievements still fresh in the memory, a scoreline so dominant followed that Middlesbrough would abstain from the competition the following season in order to give other teams a chance. A humbling 8-1 defeat saw Redcar and Coatham plummet back to reality, and Redcar Crusaders were fast becoming equals with their town counterparts.

It is at this point in time that the two clubs came together to discuss a merger, thinking that two clubs in such a small town would struggle to play competitively alongside one another. On 13th November 1886, both teams were due to compete in the first round of the Cleveland Cup. When Redcar took the field at South Bank with a much-changed side, they refused to play unless their opponents agreed to classify the game as a friendly. "The South Bank team were naturally much annoyed at this treatment; but, in order to prevent disappointment to the spectators, agreed to play,"[57] said one report. Back in Redcar, some far more familiar names were wearing the black and white halves of the Crusaders. Some of Redcar's best players had played a 20-minute long match against South Stockton a few days previously in order to qualify for the competition, and so James Howcroft, George McCrie, Tom Alvey, Bob Agar, Addison Fidler and George Hikeley, all of whom had achieved so much for the town's other side, outclassed Middlesbrough Swifts to put Crusaders into the next round.

The decision to scratch one team in favour of another was met with fierce criticism and earned Redcar a fine for unsportsmanlike conduct. It also led to something of a spat between the town's two up-and-coming football administrators; James Howcroft, who was spending more of his time chairing the Cleveland FA, and Harry Walker, who began a lifelong connection with Middlesbrough Football Club as a young man and would be a key proponent in their election to the Football League. It began when Howcroft wrote to *The Northern Echo* to explain the situation. "The Redcar Crusaders and the Redcar Club have for some time existed side by side in Redcar, having members belonging to both clubs," he said. "It has long been felt that it was a source of weakness to have forces divided in so small a place." He asked how it was possible for them to have incurred a fine for unsportsmanlike conduct when there was a precedent for amalgamating two teams in a town, as seen by Middlesbrough St John's becoming part of Middlesbrough FC. "After amalgamating it will be evident that we were compelled to scratch to South Bank in order not to disqualify our players,"[58] Howcroft concluded.

A few days later came Walker's response. "I think the letter of Mr Howcroft...scarcely gives a correct representation of the case," he began. Walker had chaired the Cleveland FA meeting in which Redcar were given a fine for unsportsmanlike conduct, and recalls asking Tom Alvey and George McCrie whether an amalgamation had taken place, to which they both replied that it had. "The question was also asked 'what is the name of the club under the amalgamation?' To this no very distinct reply was tendered, but an effort was made to explain that the two clubs had only amalgamated for the purposes of the cup competition," Walker continued. He noted that when two clubs merge, it is an inevitability that one of the clubs then ceases to exist, but that had not happened in this case. "What is its name? If it is the Crusaders, then they are not qualified to play in the English Cup competition. If it is Redcar proper, then they were not qualified to play in the first round of the Cleveland Cup competition against the Middlesbrough Swifts."[59] As a result of the controversy it has caused, the merger was abandoned, but the damage had been done.

•

> Come, pull yourselves together; make the best of your Crusader reinforcement. Wake up, McCrie and Alvey, and do your level best for "the town that owns ye."

Saltburn Times, 30th September 1887

The football world had changed immeasurably since Redcar's formation only nine years previously. The northern working classes had gained superiority over the public school Old Boys who had codified the game a few decades before. It wouldn't be until 1900 that a Southern team competed in the FA Cup final again, where Bury demolished Southampton 4-0. On the subject of FA Cup finals, the five or six thousand people who attended the finals in the late 1870s were now 20,000 strong by 1887. Professionalism in football had been legal for two years (although players had likely been paid on the sly for a few years before that), which paved the way for rich businessmen to take control of football clubs in an attempt to bring in the most talented players and, in turn, success (you wouldn't see that sort of thing happening today, of course).

Unfortunately, this splinter is where Redcar started to separate from the pack. Football had started to move away from the genteel recreation sport played at cricket clubs by schoolmasters with Cambridge degrees, politely applauded by the middle classes. Instead it turned towards a bastion of the working men who had suddenly found themselves free on Saturday afternoons. The bigger towns with a booming infrastructure and passionate local pride became the obvious hotbeds for teams that would demand more and more success. And plucky old Redcar could just no longer keep up. Only a few years previously they were demanding national attention, but now was the time that they would start looking a little closer to home.

Things weren't going to get much better. The damage that the failed merger had done seemed irreparable. "We have heard nothing about the Redcar team...but ominous and ugly whispers of internal dissension and resignations,"[60] wrote *The Saltburn Times*. After a long and successful career between the sticks, James Howcroft decided to hang up his boots. "He has achieved distinction throughout the whole of the North of England as a goalkeeper," wrote *The York Herald*, "and his assistance in many ways has been invaluable." Tom Bradbury, one of the finest backs in the county, elected to leave the team for his old club South Bank, and their captain Tom Alvey also departed. "Few men have deserved better of their club than Tom Alvey," wrote *The Northern Review*. "Alvey has been the safest and most powerful member of the team for a considerable time." An athletic and reliable player who had moved to the North East from Sheffield after playing at Pyebank, Alvey was also a popular and genial man. "The best full back Cleveland has produced"[61] had turned heads at Middlesbrough and he could ignore their calls no longer.

George McCrie and his Middlesbrough team in the Cleveland Cup final
Northern Review, 17th March 1888

Alvey spent the next few seasons primarily playing for Boro, and even joined the likes of Jackson Ewbank and Albert Borrie in lifting the Cleveland Cup after beating Redcar in the final. On this occasion though, it was the cricket team he was representing, but one player to leave the Redcar team did see cup final success with the Middlesbrough football side. George McCrie represented Boro when they resumed Cleveland Cup affairs after taking a sabbatical in the 1886/87 season, beating Stockton 3-0 in 1888. He had been a mainstay in the team throughout 1887/88, unexpectedly impressing the committee enough with his goalscoring abilities from half back that he played as a centre forward in a game against Darlington. Realising they could taste success elsewhere, there was an exodus at the club.

"What a falling off there seems to be at Redcar!" wrote *The York Herald* in 1887, "a few seasons ago it held a proud place among North of England football teams; now it is starting the season a third or fourth rate club."[62] Similar sentiments were written in *The Northern Review* around the same time: "Poor Redcar, what a fall it has sustained since the day when it claimed to be the best club in the district, bar none."[63] So how could they have gone from the last eight of the FA Cup to total mediocrity in little over a year? Lack of support from the town undeniably played a huge part, the masses instead choosing to spend their time watching the more successful Middlesbrough side in action. Internal friction had also been eating away at the club from within, the signs of years of civil war finally beginning to reveal the irreparable damage it had caused as players looked elsewhere to spend their Saturday afternoons.

They also relied heavily on the performances of one or two standout players; from Howcroft and Harrison in the early years, they then looked at club captains Tom Alvey and George McCrie, all of whom had now departed. Part of this was the result of the style of play they employed. Although the "Scotch Professor" passing game was beginning to take hold in England, many early teams south of the border employed a dribbling style of play, as opposed to the combination play of their Scottish counterparts where passing and teamwork was key. Teamwork was something that the Redcar team was lacking in, and they could no longer hide behind the individual brilliance of a select few.

The freefall at Redcar and Coatham gave Redcar Crusaders an opportunity to show the town what they could do, and the 1886/87 season saw them compete in the Cleveland Challenge Cup for the first time. Their third round game against Darlington was threatened to be postponed due to the freezing January weather, but many fans and officials had worked hard to clear the snow and felt as though the game could go ahead.

This particular moment in time is noteworthy for several reasons, beginning with the first point: The initial match. Darlington showed their superiority in the first half, scoring three goals in quick succession and seemingly putting the game out of reach.

However, Crusaders came out fighting in the second half and refused to go down without a fight. After pulling a goal back, they immediately doubled their tally to bring the game firmly back within their reach. "Great excitement now prevailed"[64] and Redcar were reliant on hope. Unfortunately, Hope played for Darlington and he scored their fourth goal, with the score finishing 4-2. Now, this is quite interesting, but there's far, far more to it.

Not least because the referee, for reasons that no-one ever quite got to the bottom of, blew for full-time a full five minutes early. Crusaders were full of righteous indignation at the transgression, as were the fans. "It would have been hard on the Crusaders to have the match decided against them when five minutes remained to be played," wrote *The Northern Review*, "if there was the slightest probability of their saving themselves from defeat."[65] The match was ordered to be replayed, which naturally wasn't a popular decision with the Darlington fans, especially since star player George Millar was due to be playing for Middlesbrough on the rearranged date, and Tom Alvey was back in contention to play for Redcar after suffering an injury that had ruled him out of the initial encounter.

Another noteworthy feature of the game was Darlington's goalkeeper. He isn't a household name for most, and his senior career doesn't scream 'legend'; one league appearance for Ashton North End, six for Stockport County, a handful of games for Preston North End. But Arthur Wharton was a trailblazer. He began his career as an amateur with Darlington where he played alongside Redcar player AC Tofts. Wharton turned professional in 1889 when he joined Rotherham, going on to play for Sheffield United as an understudy to the legendary William 'Fatty' Foulke, and for a period of time making a claim to earn an England call-up.

That call never came, though, and many believe that racial prejudice had a part to play. That's because Arthur Wharton, born in what is now Accra, Ghana, was the world's first black professional footballer. Not only that, but he was also a successful cyclist, professional cricketer and one-time fastest man in the world. He wouldn't be recognised for his achievements for almost 100 years, though, and he died a penniless alcoholic, buried in a pauper's grave. However, he is now honoured in the shape of a statue at St George's Park, and another at the FIFA headquarters, along with a place in the English Football Hall of Fame and the excellent Arthur Wharton Foundation in Darlington, featuring a museum and a stunning mural. It's safe to say that no-one else in the 1887 match between Redcar and Darlington went on to garner so much recognition.

The final point is what happened in the rearranged game. With all of the drama that had surrounded the climax (or lack thereof) of the initial match, tensions were running high: "The appearance of a Crusaders jersey having a similar influence upon the Darlington crowd to that of the proverbial red flag before the mad bull."[66] Play was evenly matched for the majority of the first half and Redcar's defence was resilient thanks to the Middlesbrough pairing of Alvey and McCrie assisting their old town, despite Alvey's ankle injury rendering him "practically a one-legged man."

Then within five minutes of half-time - when presumably the referee was considering blowing the whistle - Darlington went 1-0 up. "A roar of cheering went up, such as probably never was heard on the same ground before." That's when things started to turn nasty. Smeddle, Darlington's captain of all people, was accused of giving a Redcar player a clean right hook. Naturally, the Redcar fans didn't take too kindly to this and stormed the pitch, with the police called to break up the fracas. It's a good thing they showed up, because at full-time the home supporters decided to give some retaliation to the Redcar fans. An enquiry into Smeddle's punch deemed it "accidental" and the player faced no repercussions, and Redcar's fans also appear not to have faced any consequences for their part in the melee. The damage had been done, though, and for the first time ever there would be no Redcar team in the final of the Cleveland Challenge Cup.

●

The 1887/88 season was uneventful for the Redcar teams, with the likes of Tom Alvey, George McCrie and the Pauls brothers choosing instead to ply their trade at Middlesbrough. In November 1887, Redcar faced North Skelton at home on the Coatham Cricket Field. Skelton had severe personnel problems, arriving with no fewer than five members of their second team to fill the gaps. With that in mind, the 2-0 defeat that Redcar suffered goes some way to show the freefall that the team were in just months after their historic FA Cup appearance. Later in the month they suffered a shock defeat to Yarm. "It would seem as though fortune had altogether forsaken the seasiders," wrote *The Northern Review* of the loss, "and the once famous team doomed to be reckoned as only a third rater, nay, hardly that."[67] A similar fate would meet them in the FA Cup when although they were "expected to do great things"[68] against Sheffield Heeley in the first qualifying round, they lost 6-1.

The following season, Redcar and Coatham would also find themselves up against St Augustines in the Cleveland Challenge Cup, but it wouldn't be in the third round. Despite neither side showing anything resembling decent form in their ordinary matches throughout the year, they both conspired to reach the final in 1889 and, not only that, but Redcar reached the encounter by achieving something that they had never done in the competition: they beat Middlesbrough.

It did not pass without incident. As so many times before, the players arrived at Middlesbrough's Linthorpe Road ground in freezing conditions. Such was the condition of ground, which was "as hard as adamant,"[69] that both teams protested against playing. The referee, Dr Wilson of Birtley, had to make a decision as to whether the game should go ahead as planned or to downgrade it to a friendly. He made the decision to play for a few minutes to see how the players fared, and by half-time "it was understood that the tie was being played."

Added to the icy pitch was a strong wind that hindered any attempt at either passing or shooting, two quite important factors of a football match. The deadlock wasn't broken until two minutes before the call of time, when yet more controversy followed. The ball was "rushed between the posts by Redcar, but immediately returned." It wasn't immediately clear if the ball had crossed the line, with the referee eventually coming to the decision that it was no goal. His umpires, furiously supported by the crowd behind the goal, disagreed. After more deliberation, the referee's decision was overturned and the goal stood, followed immediately by the full-time whistle.

Understandably aggrieved, Middlesbrough took the matter to the Cleveland Football Association. At the committee meeting, it was judged that Middlesbrough had not lodged a formal complaint about the conditions of the ground and therefore the match should be considered a cup tie, the referee's decision final and Redcar the victors. Middlesbrough's response was severe. At a sparsely attended meeting of club committee members, they voted to not only cut all ties with the Cleveland Football Association but to arrange an exhibition match at the exact time and date of the Cleveland Cup final in an attempt to spoil the gate. "Could anything be more pitiful or unsportsmanlike?"[70] wrote *The Northern Echo*.

Fans arriving at the Cleveland Cup final between Redcar and Darlington St Augustines
Northern Review, 16th March 1889

With the dominant team in the area safely dispatched and left to play a friendly instead, surely after all the hard luck that met Redcar and Coatham in their five finals, this was Redcar's time. Despite indifferent form throughout the regular season, their team was a strong one; George McCrie, who had returned from his exploits with Middlesbrough, Bob Agar, Henry Stickreth and Addison Fidler were joined by Charles Pauls, just months before his debut in Preston North End's victorious Football League campaign.

In contrast to the semi-final, beautiful weather met the two teams as they entered the field at Stockton's brand new Victoria Ground which had opened just months before. Redcar started the match with the sun behind them, the wind blowing across them towards the stands. Play was open in the first half, with both teams having chances to open the scoring until an almighty scramble in front of the Saints goalkeeper somehow ended up with the ball in the net and Redcar 1-0 up.

Sketches from the 1889 Cleveland Cup final
Northern Review, 16th March 1889

St Augustines were favourites, though, and launched attack after attack at Redcar's goal. George McCrie, Redcar's captain and only frequent member of the Cleveland representative side, defended "most stubbornly."[71] But he couldn't do it all on his own, and after the Redcar keeper parried a shot from Scotsman Willie Nolli, founder of St Augustines, O'Hara had an easy job of levelling the game.

The floodgates opened from there, despite Charles Pauls' attacks as he "sped along the wing like a greyhound." A two minute double salvo followed for Darlington, with two more in the second half seeing the Saints 5-1 up. The crowd burst through the boundary ropes to celebrate, hundreds of fans entering the field in joyous celebration, only to be told that the game hadn't finished yet and they needed to leave the pitch. Play continued for a few moments longer, but the game had been long out of reach for Redcar. Willie Nolli collected the trophy for Darlington, with 2,000 people greeting them at Bank Top station when they returned home, Nolli being "carried shoulder high" into the centre of town.

Despite a prestigious cup final appearance, there was very little else for Redcar to shout about. Around the same time as the Cleveland Cup final was a match between Cleveland and Northumberland. Only a couple of years previously the Cleveland side was almost entirely made up of either Redcar or Middlesbrough players, but by 1889 there was not a single representative from the town in the squad. *The Sheffield Telegraph* declared that Redcar had simply been unable to replace William Harrison since his departure to the South. "The glory of Redcar has departed,"[72] they said.

Chapter 4: Loss

The Football League was formed in 1888, paving the way for more league competitions across the country, including the North Eastern League (inconsistently known as the North Eastern Counties League) which had its inaugural season in 1889/90. This was in addition to the Northern League, which had formed allegedly on the same day. In fact, the North Eastern League began their season a week before the Northern League, making it the region's first ever league. Featuring the likes of Middlesbrough, South Bank, Darlington and both the Newcastle teams that went on to form Newcastle United, there was no doubt that the Northern League were the heavy hitters in the region, with the NEL representing the best of the rest, including many newly-formed sides. In total, they had 10 teams for their first season; Bishop Auckland Church Institute, Shankhouse Black Watch, Port Clarence, Rendel, Whitburn, West Hartlepool, Gateshead NER, Barnard Castle, Morpeth Harriers and Birtley.

In May 1888, the North Eastern League held a meeting at the Three Tuns in Durham, where Birtley stated that they had retired from the league, going on to take part in the Northern League instead. It was here that Redcar were elected to take their place. It's strange to think that a team of Redcar's stature almost went the season without competing in any league whatsoever, and goes some way to explaining the decline the club were experiencing by 1889.

Before the season began, an optimistic article was printed in *The Gazette* singing the praises of league football and its potential to outclass any season which had come before it:

"Judging from the excellent list of fixtures which the various clubs in Cleveland and South Durham have arranged there is every prospect of the present season being not only more interesting, but far more successful than any previous season...The toughest fights will be the wrestling for supremacy in the Northern and North Eastern Leagues."
[73]

It was certainly interesting. Their first game against Church Institute was actually postponed because the carnival was coming to town. But the carnival was just beginning. Redcar's team was nothing like the old guard from the early days; James Howcroft was presiding over the Cleveland FA and was carving out an impressive career in football administration and would be elected president of the Cleveland Football Association in 1891. Former captain and Cleveland Cup winner with Middlesbrough George McCrie had sailed to America in May 1889. Defensive stalwart Bob Agar had recently revealed that he would be parting ways with the club, and his announcement was met with a passionate fan letter published in the *Gazette* entitled 'A Redcar Old Player':

Bob Agar
Sports Gazette, 22nd March 1924

"For the last seven, eight, or nine seasons he has taken up his position on the field in the Cleveland and English Cup ties in which his club has been engaged without, to my knowledge, a single failure; never absent, and not only there, but able to give a good account of himself. At his best he was anything but a 'light to the feet and a lamp in the path' of his opponents, to which some of the best forwards Middlesbrough ever possessed could swear." [74]

Sadly, there would also be more permanent losses to Redcar's football heritage. Just days after playing in Redcar's 5-1 defeat to St Augustines in the Cleveland Cup final, Addison Fidler, a mainstay in the team for the better part of a decade, died at his home aged just 29.

Then, one autumnal morning in Kent in October 1889, William Harrison woke from his bed, damp with sweat. What followed, as it had done so often, was the cough. He had struggled to shake it, no matter what remedies he tried, so he paid a visit to the doctor. There he learned the devastating news that so many people at this time had been hearing: He was suffering from consumption. The disease now known as tuberculosis had no known cure until antibiotics were discovered decades later, so treatment came in the form of cod liver oil, vinegar massages and the inhalation of things like hemlock and turpentine.[75]

A change of air was also considered to be an important part of recovery in Victorian times, and with TB becoming out of control by the 1880s it was common for members of the middle classes to be sent to foreign dependencies for treatment. During the mid-1800s, an estimated 90% of all Britons who were traveling due to ill health were suffering from tuberculosis.[76] And so it was that William Harrison boarded a ship headed for South Africa on 1st November 1889, his destination being the remote town of Smithfield in what was then known as the Orange Free State. He stayed there for a little over four months, every day hoping to start on the road to recovery so that he might return home and resume his government inspectorship role.

In the pre-antibiotic era, patients who were sent for a change of air were done so as a palliative measure; they would travel somewhere to make them as comfortable as possible with the intention of giving the body the best chance at healing itself. For William, every day would be the same; he would wake, he would walk along the Caledon River to take in the clean air, then he would rest in his bed and hope the new day would be better than the last. Wake, walk, rest. Wake, walk, rest. Until 17th April 1890 when the new day didn't come.

At the age of 32, far from his home in a land he didn't know, William Harrison died. He had few possessions with him in the simple South African hotel room that had been his home for nearly half a year, mostly clothes and money. But one item on his probate stands out: A valuable pocket watch. It's tempting to imagine that it was the same gold watch that was presented to him in 1884 in recognition of his services to Redcar, and the memento by his bedside helped him recall those halcyon days where he helped establish the club, however briefly, as one of the finest teams in the North of England, and that those memories acted as a light in his darkest days.

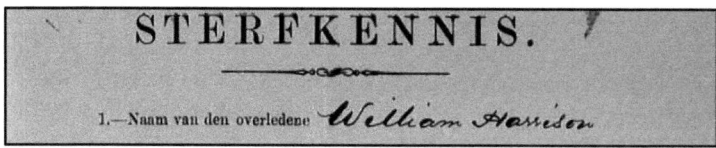

William Harrison's probate[77]

News of his untimely demise reached English newspapers around a week later, where his death was mourned not only in Redcar but in Sheffield where he had done such good service for the Sheffield Association side as well as Sheffield Wednesday. "There are few players who can boast of such a brilliant brief football career as the deceased," wrote *The Sheffield Evening Telegraph*, "his was the old school style of play, naturally fast on the ball and dodgy, but with these qualities unselfishness was combined, making him a tower of strength to his side and a terror to his opponents." Not just a great footballer, Harrison was the model of a great man who gave thoughtful advice both on and off the pitch, "of a loveable disposition, large hearted, and kindly to all, the news of his decease will be received with regret by a large circle of acquaintances."[78] Many players have represented Redcar and gone on to great things, but no Redcar player will ever achieve what William Harrison did whilst still an active member of the club. His name should be spoken about alongside the very best footballers that the town has ever produced.

•

The loss of Harrison and Fidler, as well as the other legends who had departed the club, was felt heavily by Redcar's North Eastern League side. Without five first-choice players, they travelled to Whitburn in their second planned fixture. Despite their disadvantage, they played well in the first half and went into half-time 2-1 up. But the second half was not so forgiving. Whitburn showed a superiority and fighting spirit that would bring them great success throughout the season and managed to score four goals without reply, the match ending 5-2 to the home side. By October when the return fixture came around, *The Morpeth Herald* summed up what Redcar's reputation in the competition had become: "On Saturday, Whitburn went to Redcar, and gave the home team a regular thrashing, scoring five goals to none."[79]

Thrashings were indeed regular. A 5-0 loss against Port Clarence, 4-0 against West Hartlepool, and 4-1 against both Rendel and Barnard Castle punctuated the season. In fact, one of Redcar's few decent results came against bottom of the table West Hartlepool in December, a feat they only achieved because their opponents had requested to move the fixture as half of their squad were still on their Christmas holidays, but Redcar saw one of their few opportunities to gain some points and refused to change the date. The game went ahead and Redcar, playing against mostly juniors and reserves, won 4-0.

Several newspapers reported that the North Eastern League was going to draw to a close on 26th April, as was planned in the fixture list released at the start of the season. However, by the time the clubs' end of season annual meetings rolled around in May and June, many of the fixtures were yet to be fulfilled. In fact, it would appear that Whitburn just simply assumed that they won the league, despite not being sure if it was officially over:

"In the North Eastern Counties League so far as the competition had been carried out, the team headed the list, their record being 10 won, five lost, one drawn, making a total of 21 points."[80]

This end of season retrospective mentions a total of 16 games, despite the fact that they should have played 18. Port Clarence were four games behind Whitburn by the end of the season, but had only won two fewer games, and if they won their games in hand they could have easily leapfrogged Whitburn. Redcar were in no danger of winning the league, but West Hartlepool's game in hand at the bottom of the table could have meant that Redcar finished dead last if the fixtures were played out. Rendel's secretary, at their own annual meeting in May, sums up the attitude towards the way the league turned out in its first season in stark contrast to the letter published in the *Gazette* in the Summer of 1889:

"I do not think that the most ardent advocate of the Leagues can say that the North Eastern League has been a success. I myself have been disappointed. I thought when it was first mooted that it was a very good thing, that it would get fixtures kept, and each club would do their best to make it a success."[81]

It's clear that with cancelled games, a confusing and unclear end to the season, and some questionable attitudes from the clubs that the management of a football league was a process that was yet to be fine-tuned. In morbidly poetic fashion, the death of William Harrison had also coincided with Redcar's own demise.

It is here, at perhaps more than any other point in Redcar's footballing history, that we can ask ourselves - what if? What if they had held on to that 3-0 lead in the first Cleveland Cup final way back in 1882? Where would that momentum have taken them, and what players could have chosen to bring their talents to Redcar instead of cup champions Middlesbrough? How many more finals could they have snatched from Middlesbrough had that been the case? So, too, we could ask what if William Harrison had been available to travel to Birmingham on that historic winter afternoon against Small Heath? Could his involvement down that ineffectual right flank have turned the tide and brought Redcar an FA Cup semi-final?

What if the Football League, and by proxy, the Northern League, had come just a season or two earlier? Could Redcar have been considered for the most prestigious league in the area? The Northern League was a breeding ground for success in those days; only three years after its inaugural season, Newcastle West End and East End combined to form Newcastle United and entered the Football League, never to drop out of it. Stockton, South Bank, Middlesbrough and Bishop Auckland all went on to win the FA Amateur Cup, with Middlesbrough and Darlington going on to join Newcastle in the Football League. What if Birtley had remained in the North Eastern League, with Redcar taking their place in the Northern League instead?

In truth, without a rapid expansion of the town, considerable success would have been unlikely. The league's two smallest teams, Birtley and Elswick, finished bottom in the Northern League's first season. Up against powerhouses like Middlesbrough, 75,000 people strong, Stockton with its 60,000 population, Newcastle with 214,0000 inhabitants, and Darlington, with a population of 47,000[82] as well as towns experiencing a boom from the industrial revolution such as South Bank and Bishop Auckland, little Redcar with its barely 3,000 inhabitants would have struggled to establish themselves as long-term contenders for the highest league in the land.

Middlesbrough continued to grow during this period and presented the problem that Redcar and Coatham had experienced with Redcar Crusaders: Two teams in such a small area found it impossible to gain the same amount of success. So how could Redcar – who had positioned themselves as a seaside resort – compete for Teesside superiority with the great Ironopolis, that Infant Hercules? Such was the gulf that had grown between the two sides that in Middlesbrough's annual meeting in 1889, it was presented as a source of embarrassment to have lost to them: "The references to the defeats sustained by the premier team at the hands of Redcar, Birtley and Ecclesfield brought forth laughter and groans from the assembled members, and the secretary had 'to take a drink'."[83]

Redcar were forced to watch from the sidelines as Middlesbrough – both the town and the club - grew immeasurably over the coming years. This does not mean, though, that Redcar no longer tasted success. After beating Scarborough in a friendly in January 1890, they then dispatched Middlesbrough Milton Street Amateurs 7-0. But these results are insignificant next to what happened on 7th April 1890, when Redcar met South Bank in Middlesbrough in front of 2,000 people. This was the Cleveland Junior Cup final, and it was Redcar and Coatham's chance to finally get their hands on silverware. They had lost in the final the previous year to that season's opponents – South Bank – and had never won the competition although their town counterparts Redcar Crusaders won it in its inaugural season six years previously.

They'd faced a difficult road to get there. After beating Marske earlier in the competition, their opponents then complained to the Cleveland FA that Redcar had fielded four players over the age limit, and should therefore be disqualified. There were no birth certificates to prove it either way so, according to *The Northern Echo*, it was "left in the hands of the secretary."[84]

However the secretary came to a decision, it was in Redcar's favour, as the following week the four men were deemed to be "duly qualified"[85] and they made their way to the final. More luck greeted them when one of South Bank's star players was injured in a practice match shortly before the match. A 3-2 victory followed and Redcar and Coatham, led by former senior captain George McCrie's younger brother, finally had some silverware after 12 years.

The following Tuesday night, the club were "entertained to a complimentary dinner by a few of their admirers and supporters, in honour of winning the cup."[86] They sang songs and gave speeches, celebrating "justice having been done to the repast" and giving special thanks to the club's chairman Mr Dodds. It was mentioned that there was regret that, for reasons no one could quite explain, the trophy was not present that evening. This would not be the last time that their care of the trophy would be called into question.

Upon the resumption of the season in April 1891, the club returned the Cleveland Junior Cup damaged. The Cleveland FA wrote to Redcar about it but received no response. It was therefore decided that they would send the trophy to a local jeweller for repair and send Redcar the bill. Adding insult to injury was the senior club's fine as a result of not fulfilling their fixture obligations. They said that due to financial problems they could not pay the debt, and they were therefore suspended until they could.

Redcar and Coatham did not re-enter the North Eastern League in 1890/91. They abandoned the league after its first season, with Gateshead NER, Rendel and Whitburn joining three Northern League teams to reform the league under the banner of the Northern Alliance. Redcar sat the season out, but they returned to league football in 1891/92 in the Cleveland Amateur League. For a time, it looked like things were looking up for a team who seemed like their best days were behind them, and there were some decent results that season; not least the 8-1 destruction of Loftus and a 6-0 drubbing of Guisborough (which was slightly overshadowed by Whitby winning 13-0 on the same day). But these were not the glory years for Redcar and Coatham.

James Howcroft's career, though, was just beginning. After years of dedication to chairing the Cleveland FA, it was time for a new challenge. The Football Association Council was made up of representatives of each region of the country, with the North Eastern Division being represented by Darlington FC founder Charles Craven. But by 1890, Howcroft "consented to be put in nomination" for the post after Craven had moved to Leeds to start the development of Headingley Cricket Ground. "If I know anything of footballers on Teesside at all," the article continued, "I think they can be relied upon to plump for Mr Howcroft to a man." He had earned himself a stellar reputation in the region, not only for his kind and genial nature but his "manly attitude, sound common sense, and justness,"[87] and for his sheer love of the game. "I do not fear but that the interests of the clubs throughout the division will be served with satisfaction to all should he be returned, of which I have every confidence."[88]

So in 1891, James Howcroft was elected onto the Football Association Council, representing the North Riding in the highest footballing office in the land. Through hard work and dedication to the Beautiful Game he had not only gained himself a reputation as one of the finest amateur goalkeepers of his time, he was also carving out a career as one of the most respected administrators in the game.

•

The Redcar team found themselves being spoken about in the press up and down the country in March 1893, just like they were a decade previously, but this time for all the wrong reasons. The team, who were going by the name Redcar and Coatham United, were on their way back from a Cleveland Amateur League match against Guisborough. The driver of the team coach lost control as it travelled down a bank at Dunsdale, about halfway between the two towns. It careered into a wall, flinging its occupants out on impact. Dawkings, former goalkeeping star of both Middlesbrough's FA Cup quarter-final team and the Cleveland representative side, as well as the thorn in Redcar's side for so many Cleveland Cup final defeats, broke his leg and never played again. John Anderson, who won the Cleveland Junior Cup with Redcar in 1890, broke one of his ribs.

A month later, as the Cleveland Amateur League and Teesside League both drew to a close, representatives of teams from both leagues played a benefit match for Dawkings, for whom they raised £5, over £600 in today's money. It is hard to argue that the final league standings were a success for Redcar. They finished seventh out of nine places, winning four, drawing one and losing 10. They conceded 61 goals over the season, although it was somewhat eclipsed by Guisborough who conceded 90.

By the following season, Redcar were competing in the Teesside League. It did not go well. The *Gazette* wondered how they would fare against Thornaby Excelsior, as "at their last meeting they got an overwhelming thrashing."[89] They lost 1-0, which kept them rooted to the bottom of the table having lost all five of their games. On 9th October, *The York Herald* printed the following:

"The association game is in a very poor way at Redcar compared with what it was a few years ago, and as a result of the 13-0 defeat a fortnight ago the Redcar and Coatham Club is making a determined attempt to get a respectable team together."[90]

They failed to get a respectable team together and withdrew from the Teesside League. It was not a popular decision. They were terrible, granted, but on top of outstanding subscriptions still owed to the league, there were clubs in the division that paid a fair amount of cash to travel to Redcar and as a result of them withdrawing would see no return for it if the reverse fixtures were not fulfilled. These problems seemed insurmountable for the Redcar committee, and as a result they made a gut-wrenching decision. The club was to disband.

Just 17 years after the cricketers at Redcar and Coatham YMCA decided to take up a new sport to fill the winter months, the club had gone. The seeds had been sewn since the mid-1880s, manifested in internal conflict, poor behaviour and terrible form. Coinciding with the beginnings of league football to which they struggled to adapt, Redcar and Coatham were on a downward spiral which saw them fall further and further from their national recognition they had earned only a few years previously, to the point that they could hardly be considered notable even in Cleveland. They left such a mark on the game in the early days, it's disappointing for them to have bowed out not with a bang but with a whimper.

The team and their achievements were looked upon as a flash in a pan, already appearing antiquated after the formations of leagues featuring professional players throughout the country. They became a distant memory, only occasionally mentioned in passing when a member of that old team happened to appear in the local press. Over 140 years later, knowledge of the club barely registers on local historians' radars, an unknown to the town's inhabitants. Middlesbrough's fierce rivals became Stockton, who would become such a force in amateur football for years to come. No sign of football is left behind at the cricket club, and the site of their first home at Redcar Racecourse was turned into a supermarket. Redcar may have all but forgotten what the club achieved and the national esteem in which they were once held, but they should be proud that for a brief moment in time they were spoken about alongside the very best teams in world football, "as good as anything in the country."[91]

Chapter 5: Custodians

As the pulse of Redcar and Coatham faltered, some of the old guard were only at the beginning of their journey. James Howcroft was in his mid-40s by 1895 and it had been six years since he had hung up his boots. But Howcroft, a tireless worker, knew nothing of the word 'retirement' and he remained in football for the rest of his life. After bringing Redcar to national attention in the early 1880s, he knew his job wasn't done. A quiet individual who kept away from the limelight despite his continuing determination to make a stamp on the sport, Howcroft remained close to the game by refereeing and running the line at many notable matches once his playing days were over, in which he "proved far above the average in ability."[92]

His talents were so in demand that he was often booked to referee matches six weeks before the game. His fee for officiating Middlesbrough matches was increased by 4d by chairman - and one-time rival - Fred Hardisty such was the esteem in which he was held. By 1895, he'd earned such a good reputation that he was selected to be a linesman at three consecutive FA Cup finals; the 1895 final between Aston Villa and West Brom, Wednesday vs Wolves in 1896 and Aston Villa vs Everton in 1897, the latter being in front of a crowd of 65,000.

James Howcroft (back to camera) acting as linesman at the 1896 FA Cup final
Courtesy of Clive Nicholson

Howcroft never officiated a Football League game, despite gaining plaudits for handling FA Cup matches such as a fiercely-contested tie between Newcastle and Bolton. He was repeatedly told that "he only had an application to make" but believed that such a prerequisite should not be needed, and ability should speak for itself. "Kissing, we are told, goes by favour, and so do most of our football appointments," an article discussing Howcroft's refereeing career concluded.

The gap left by Redcar and Coatham on the local footballing landscape by the 1890s paved the way for smaller teams to take their place. The middle of the decade saw some new kids who were very briefly on the block. Not even really on the block, just hanging around. Passing through. They were army teams. One of them was the Redcar F Company Volunteers, who showed up briefly to beat Redcar's A Team 6-0, then disappear again. There was also the Princess of Wales' Own Volunteers of Redcar, who played in the South Bank Challenge Cup – now known as the Ellis Cup - in 1896, beating Thornaby East End at the Normanby Ground on the way to knocking South Bank Wednesday out in the semi-final. They met South Bank Juniors in the final, who had won the trophy five times in the competition's first seven years. Unfortunately for Redcar, they made it six from eight in the 1896 final.

By 1898, Redcar Crusaders were on the up. They were competing in the Cleveland Amateur League, and the previous season had made their debut in the FA Amateur Cup, going on to make sporadic appearances in the competition until 1908. Newly-formed Redcar and Coatham Rovers, although reporting a loss on their finances, had a good season. Their annual meeting stated that they played 13 matches, winning 10, drawing two and only losing once. They'd reached the Cleveland Junior Cup final in 1897 and lost to a strong South Bank junior side after extra time (although they contested the result as they had to play the remainder of the game with 10 men), but they won the trophy in 1898. Club colours were also decided, drawing another line under the original club by taking a departure from the black and red and instead adopting the horse racing colours of Wilton Castle's owner James Lowther MP, which were dark blue and yellow hoops.

The junior side continued to show their cup pedigree in 1899, beating Brotton Albion in the semi-finals to tee up a final against South Bank once again. This time the Bankers didn't need extra time, and walloped Redcar 7-0 in front of upwards of 2,000 spectators. This was to be the last game of any note played under the banner of Redcar and Coatham Rovers. They did not reappear in the 1899/1900 season, all the while the town's second team, Redcar Crusaders, went about their business.

Crusaders, always challengers in the Cleveland Junior Cup, would also see proof of the quality of their youngsters in the coming years when players would go on to see success that the Redcar club could only dream of, when a young goalkeeper had such a good game that he immediately attracted the attention of some high-profile suitors.

Reginald Garnet Williamson, nicknamed Tim on account of his small stature for a goalkeeper (Tiny Tim, get it?) was 16 years old when Redcar Crusaders reached yet another Cleveland Junior Cup final in 1900. The final pitted them against perennial finalists South Bank, who would not only go on to win the FA Amateur Cup in 1913, but would also produce some of the best players in the region for years to come. South Bank *were* the Cleveland Junior Cup, and they had a youth team that could rival any in the country. When they met Redcar Crusaders in the replayed Junior Cup tie in April 1900, they won it again, despite the best efforts of the Redcar fans offering their bit of gamesmanship:

Tim Williamson
Pinnace football card, Godfrey Phillips Ltd, 1922

"A number of the Redcar supporters on the covered stand were specially [sic] boisterous, and the way they hooted the referee whenever a decision was not in their favour was most ungentlemanly."

It was to no avail, however, as South Bank convincingly won the game 4-0. But what is interesting about the game is the fact that The Northern Echo repeatedly pointed out Redcar's goalkeeper Tim Williamson, whom they practically structured their entire match report around, to note that not only should he be spared from blamed for the loss, but that he should be praised for his performance:

"A specially [sic] hard man to pass was the goalkeeper, Williamson, who played what was admittedly one of the best games ever seen in a local junior final...the first goal, he had no chance to save, and in at least two of the three goals scored in the second period it was the fault of the full back, and not of Williamson." [93]

Williamson's first notable foray into the world of football came at Coatham Grammar School, where he actually started out as a forward. At some point during this time he tried his hand at goalkeeping and quickly earned himself a reputation. As *The Sheffield Daily Telegraph* put it in a piece entitled 'Middlesbro's Custodian', he:

"First played football with Redcar Grammar School, where he gained such an excellent reputation for his custodianship that he was persuaded to do duty for Redcar Crusaders. His play in the Cleveland Association's Junior Cup competition brought his splendid abilities under the notice of the Middlesbrough Club."

Barely 18 years of age, he had already done enough to catch the eye of a Football League team, famously playing for Redcar Crusaders in the morning and then appearing for Middlesbrough in a friendly against Cliftonville in the afternoon. But it wasn't all plain sailing from there, as the teenager had to compete with Scottish international Rab Mcfarlane for a place in the squad. His first season was mostly spent with their A team, who competed in the Northern Football Alliance, but it didn't take long to get a Football League debut, his introduction to the first team coming in April 1902. It went pretty well. "He made his debut in higher-class football," wrote *The Sheffield Daily Telegraph* the following year, "and with such credit, that the Middlesbrough club had no hesitation in retaining his services for the present season."[94]

By the 1903/04 season, at just 19 years old, he was a first team regular with Middlesbrough. At this point in time you could open a random match report and see a line gushing about Williamson's performances. Take *Athletic News* in November 1905: "The position seemed hopeless, but 'Tim' at once gave evidence of his powers of divination and anticipating the movement of Liverpool's inside right brought off a wonderful save. Again and again did the Redcar youth cover himself with glory by his heroic defence."[95]

When the 1912/13 FA Cup campaign began, *The Green 'un* ran profile snapshots on key players. On the right-hand side of the page were Chelsea players and on the left were Boro players. The very top space was reserved for the two clubs' superstars. Chelsea's was Jock Cameron, their stalwart captain and a Scotland international. Boro's, of course, was Williamson. After briefly mentioning his Redcar Crusaders career, his profile ended by saying simply "no better goalkeeper in Great Britain."[96] The international select committee (featuring Redcar's Harry Walker) agreed, earning seven full England caps across his long career.

As the 1913/14 season drew to a close, conflict overseas could not be ignored any longer and professional football ceased operations. Williamson's job as a draughtsman meant that he was exempt, ironically, from being drafted but he worked in a munitions factory in Sheffield, during which time Wednesday - with echoes of William Harrison in the 1880s - were keen to have him on board.

Upon his return to football in 1919 he was briefly dropped from the Middlesbrough squad. His replacement was Harry Harrison, having waited in the shadows since moving up from amateur football in Redcar himself. He had a couple more shots before Williamson was reinstated, but Harrison was happy to play the long game. By 1922, Williamson came down with a nasty case of influenza which kept him out for the season, and once again Harrison stepped up. By this season, both of Middlesbrough's goalkeepers had come from Redcar, and their star striker George Elliott was also an ex-Crusaders man.

Harry Harrison in goal for Middlesbrough Reserves
Sports Gazette, 27th August 1921

Despite the breaks for a world war and severe illness, Williamson managed 130 consecutive appearances on the way to playing for Middlesbrough 602 times, even managing two goals. The only person that has ever got remotely close to him was Gordon Jones half a century later, who notched up 527 total appearances. It's unlikely that Tim's record will ever be broken, even though his career had been so heavily truncated by illness and war.

Williamson eventually retired in 1923 just shy of 40 years old. *The Newcastle Journal* wrote that upon his retirement: "Local sportsmen made him a public presentation for he was the idol of the crowd during some of the club's most anxious years."[97] He stayed away from football in the subsequent years, taking up golf as his main pastime, and he'd given so much to the game that no-one could blame him for taking a step back. On 1st August 1943, Williamson died at the age of 59 following an operation. He is buried in Coatham Churchyard. In his obituary, *The Hartlepool Mail* called him the "greatest of all Middlesbrough goalkeepers,"[98] a fact that very few could argue.

•

By 1902, as Williamson was making his case to step up to Middlesbrough's senior team, Redcar Crusaders were playing in the Cleveland Alliance League and would stay there for the next few years. They reached the final of the Cleveland Junior Cup – by then briefly referred to as the North Riding and Teesside Junior Cup – and once again lost to South Bank, as they had done so many times before.

Although the glory years of Harrison, Howcroft, Alvey et al were a distant memory, and most of Redcar's current top players were not even born when that team historically reached the quarter-finals of the FA Cup, Redcar would have a hand in the 1905 FA Cup final. That's because Newcastle, one of that year's finalists, trained at Redcar before travelling down to London. As a strange quirk of fate, their opponents Aston Villa had themselves been staying in Redcar, using it as a base when fulfilling their league fixtures against Newcastle and Middlesbrough earlier in the month.

Newcastle lost the game, however, despite being tipped as favourites by many publications. In fact, many articles previewing the final seemed to make some bold suggestions that the stiff breeze from the North Sea would somehow energise them and spur them on to victory. It wasn't to be for Newcastle, even with the advantage of fresh salt air in their lungs, and Aston Villa won 2-0.

By 1905, Redcar were competing in the Cleveland Alliance League against the likes of Saltburn, Skinningrove and Loftus. They also competed in the FA Amateur Cup in 1906, playing against league compatriots Skinningrove in the third round. The game took place in torrential downpour on a miserable November afternoon away from home. Despite Redcar taking a convincing lead in the first half, Skinningrove came out fighting after the restart and somehow conspired to come away 4-3 winners. As an interesting side note, there were two Redcar men involved in drawing the teams that year; Harry Walker and James Howcroft, who had now established themselves as the region's top football administrators.

Such was Howcroft's influence at this point, he was literally changing the game. "I consider the goalkeeper is now too much protected by the rules," Howcroft said in an interview in 1906, "I think that as soon as he leaves his area he should be treated like an ordinary player, and not allowed to pick up the ball at all."[99] A few years later, Howcroft got his wish. "Before closing the interview," that same article finished, "Mr Howcroft also expressed himself in favour of preventing a player from being offside in his own half of the field." Howcroft's influence helped this law become a reality just one year later. It seems incredible that these laws weren't changed decades previously, and were it not for people like James Howcroft and his forward-thinking approach to the game, it would be a very different sport today. "I have spoken to several of my colleagues on these subjects," he concluded, "and they warmly support the proposals as being likely to improve the game to a very large extent." He was right.

Not really a player, Howcroft's long-term colleague Harry Walker was nonetheless a Redcar lad and did as much for local and national football as Howcroft did. Both men made an impact at a relatively young age, with Howcroft – the older of the two – being

A sketch of Harry Walker
Sports Gazette, 30th June 1928

one step ahead of Walker, who went on to become chairman of the North Riding Football Association and was subsequently elected as a vice president of the Football Association. He spent so long in the position that he was given the title of life vice president only five short months before his death. He was described as "one of the most popular men in football"[100] and not only strove to bring a higher profile to teams in the North East, but was instrumental in Middlesbrough's election in the Football League, which had been a tricky task with the disagreements with Ironopolis. He died in Redcar at the age of 81 after a short illness. Both men did an incredible amount of work to ensure that North East football was the standard it deserved to be, and their achievements should never be forgotten.

•

A few months after Redcar's 4-3 loss to Skinningrove was the draw for the North Riding Junior Cup, and it pitted Redcar Crusaders against a new team. Since 1878, with the exception of a couple of army teams who played a handful of games, there had only been two senior teams in the town of any note; the original Redcar and Coatham, and Redcar Crusaders. But the 1900s saw a rise in the number of teams as the game became a hugely popular spectator sport, meaning there was enough interest both in players good enough to compete and fans who wanted to watch it. Since the formation of the Football League in 1888, a whole manner of leagues of varying levels were sprouting up constantly in order to accommodate the influx of teams year-on-year. So in 1906, the town had another team: Redcar Zetland.

It cannot be argued that Zetland made an indelible mark on the football world, either locally or nationally. They didn't win any trophies, they didn't have an FA Cup run, their players didn't go on to change the game for the better. Rather, it's what Zetland's existence represents. The town was no longer reliant on one or two well-established sides that had the rub of the green well before the sport was as far-reaching as it was by the turn of the century. As such a minor team it's difficult to know exactly where Zetland came from, but when they were competing alongside Crusaders in the South Bank League in 1908 they were referred to as "Redcar Zetland

Old Boys," which points to them being connected to the local Zetland School. The school had long had a connection to football in Redcar, with William Harrison's brother Tom, also a member of the original team, moving from Lancaster to become their headmaster in the 1870s.

As Redcar began to establish more sides, different regions began to form their own clubs. This is where the Warrenby Wednesday team are first seen. Jacob Newell played for them in 1907, and the team went on to win the 1909 North Yorkshire and South Durham League, where the medals were presented by none other than James Howcroft. Newell was a sailor with the Royal Navy in World War I, serving on at least four warships before his death in 1930. Warrenby had a very respectable team in the 1940s and won local titles and even had the honour of playing at Ayresome Park.

Jacob Newell in a Warrenby Wednesday kit
Courtesy of Bob Newell

For the next couple of decades or so, the trend of increasing Redcar football clubs would continue. More and more minor teams would pop up around the town, most notably Redcar West End and Redcar Victoria. By 1908, Redcar Crusaders were plying their trade in the Teesside League. Crusaders also had a repeat of their FA Amateur Cup match from 1906 when they faced Skinningrove in the North Riding Amateur Cup. Although Skinningrove were unbeaten so far in the season, Crusaders were still confident of getting a result. They didn't. To be honest, they rarely did so their confidence was very much misplaced. When they visited Hartlepool later in the season, *The Hartlepool Northern Daily Mail* said: "The Seasiders are not doing well in the tournament this season, holding, as they do, one of the bottom positions."[101] Elsewhere, Redcar Zetland were competing in the South Bank League in 1907/08, but disappeared after that.

More clubs meant more players, and more players meant the greater likelihood that someone in the area would go on to bigger and better things. Such was the case with Redcar-born Bobby Simpson, a young hard-hitting right back who had been plying his trade in the town around this time before making the step up to Grangetown Athletic and South Bank. There his talents were spotted by Football League sides. After a trial with Bradford City in 1912, he signed for Everton a few days later. Initially playing in their reserve side, he broke into the first team in the 1914/15 season, making nine Football League appearances on the way to winning the First Division title, the first ex-Redcar man to do so since Charles Pauls in 1890. He also broke a long-standing curse when he helped the Toffees reach an FA Cup semi-final, eventually losing 2-0 to Chelsea. Simpson's final appearance for Everton came in April 1915 in a 2-1 win over West Brom, going on to sign for Wrexham after the conclusion of the war, taking part in their historic 1921/22 season in which they joined the Football League Division Three North before later playing for Chester.

Bobby Simpson playing for Everton in 1913/14
The Daily Citizen, n.d.

•

The town's ambitions had plummeted since the early days of national success. By the 1908/09 season, Crusaders had a team in the Teesside League, also replacing Zetland's team in the South Bank League, which had become vacant after the club's demise. Neither of them were very good. By as early as September, their Teesside League side had played five, lost five and conceded 34, scoring only four times. That amounts to losing almost every match the equivalent of 7-1. Their South Bank League side had only played once, losing it 9-1 which unsurprisingly put them bottom of the table.

Towards the end of the season, they were still bottom of the Teesside League, having won once all season. They faced a Lazenby Institute side who were sitting in fourth position, just five points behind league leaders Stockton Victoria. After an even start to the game, Lazenby took the lead when Gilbert opened the scoring with 10 minutes gone. Here we go. Then, somehow, a "bombardment of the visitors' goal followed."[102] Their persistence was rewarded when Wanless was brought down in the area and

Crusaders were given a penalty, which was duly converted. The sides went in level at half-time. They didn't let up in the second half, and resumed their bombardment. Two more goals followed, which was capped off by another shortly before the end of the game. Redcar had done it. A shock 4-1 victory saw them win only their second game all season.

A 0-0 draw against Thornaby St Patricks followed a few days later, but they had left it much too close to the end of the season for a late rally. Owing to cup competitions and bad weather, by the end of April only one team in the Teesside League had fulfilled all of their fixtures, with Eston United still needing to play 10 of their matches, which was half of their entire season's schedule. On pondering the close to the season, *The Green 'un* said: "Better late than never, but far better never late. How true this is when applied to Redcar Crusaders is obvious to all who have taken note of their recent doings."[103] It should be noted, though, that Eston's shocking fixture fulfilment owed a lot to their incredible run all the way to the FA Amateur Cup final, played at Ilford. In just two short years they would join the Northern League and win it on their first attempt, then again the following year. So although Redcar's season was not ideal, the company they were keeping were considered to be some of the finest amateur clubs in the country.

Despite some indifferent form in the local leagues, 1909 saw silverware come to the town after a long wait. The towns of Redcar and Coatham had officially amalgamated by this point, and with that in mind it's worth noting the achievements of Coatham United, who were based in what is now considered to be an area of Redcar. They won the Cleveland Junior Cup in April 1909, beating Middlesbrough St Mary's College 2-1. Between the sticks was one Harry Harrison, who would go on to play for Middlesbrough as an understudy to the legendary Tim Williamson.

They also had Stanley Borrie in the team, who was a member of the Redcar Crusaders side at the same time. Borrie had footballing pedigree, with his father Albert being a

Stanley Borrie in his Redcar days
Courtesy of Neil Harris

former Middlesbrough player who was so frequently a thorn in Redcar's side, scoring against them in the Cleveland Challenge Cup final, and going on to be secretary. Stanley's form for the Redcar sides was enough to catch the attention of Northern

League side South Bank, who took him on a few years later. Perennially on the scoresheet, Borrie inspired South Bank to an FA Amateur Cup win in 1912/13, scoring in the initial drawn game.

•

"It has been decided to form a new Amateur League for Cleveland," wrote *The Leeds Mercury* in August 1909, "and to offer a cup and also a shield for competition."[104] And just like the Teesside League, the newly-formed Cleveland League would attract some high quality opposition. "Most of the leading amateur clubs in the district, including Eston United, last season's Amateur Cup finalists, have expressed themselves favourable to the new league," continued the report. Representatives from two Redcar clubs attended the initial meeting to form the league, Redcar Victoria and Redcar Wednesday, and in fact a member of Victoria was elected to be secretary of the league, but another team from the town would find success at the end of the season.

Although Redcar Victoria got off to a very good start in the league's first division, convincingly beating Brotton Vulcan 5-0, in the league's second division a team called Redcar Celtic were impressing. Victoria and Celtic were two of the town's best teams at this point, both also featuring alongside Redcar West End in the North Riding Amateur Cup (with Victoria also playing the FA Amateur Cup the same season). Celtic competed against the likes of Lingdale Swifts, Loftus Albion and Charlton Rovers II in the Cleveland League Second Division and managed to overcome them all in a title-winning season. The winners were presented with medals made from silver with their name and 'Redcar Celtic FC' engraved into them. They may have to wait a while, but this wouldn't be the only silverware that Celtic would bring to the town.

George Elliott in his Middlesbrough kit
Sports Picture Post, 1912

Away from local leagues, another former Redcar player made a step up in the 1909/10 season, joining some men who had walked that path themselves. Tim Williamson and Harry Harrison welcomed George Elliott, a Sunderland-born centre forward, to Middlesbrough's First Division side and it didn't take long for him to make an impact. His 10 goals in 1910/11 was enough to make him Boro's top goalscorer, and he continued that trend for the next three seasons. He ended up being their top scorer in seven out of nine seasons, being the First Division's leading goalscorer in 1913/14 and breaking Middlesbrough's all-time record for most goals in a match when he scored *11* in a reserve win against Houghton Rovers.

Elliott had started his career at Redcar Crusaders, spotted playing in the Ellis Cup as a young man and moving up to the Northern League with South Bank shortly afterwards. After a successful season, he joined Middlesbrough the following year and spent his entire professional career with them, not including a guest appearance for Celtic during World War I, becoming the second former-Redcar man to wear the three lions when he made three appearances for England either side of the war. His first cap, in England's victorious British Home Championship campaign against Ireland, saw him start alongside another Crusaders star: Tim Williamson.

Elliott and Williamson weren't the only former-Redcar men to be garnering recognition on a national level during this period. James Howcroft, still hard at work as both a surveyor to Redcar Council and as a football administrator, was honoured for his hard work for both the North Riding FA and as honourable secretary for the Northern Division of the FA Amateur Cup by being presented with a long service award for over 20 years of dedication. At a meeting of the Council of the Football Association, Howcroft was given a gold medal by Lord Kinnaird, president of the FA and one-time football superstar from the days of public school dominance.

Redcar West End, 1910/11
Courtesy of Ronnie Burniston

By the end of 1910/11 season, another new Redcar team had announced themselves. Joining Crusaders, Celtic and Victoria, the town had a new addition to the Cleveland League: Redcar West End. West End first appeared in 1908, notably losing 9-2 to South Bank Victoria, also competing in the Cleveland Challenge Cup. They didn't do much of note for a couple of years, but by 1910/11 they had assembled a strong side that mounted a title challenge for the Cleveland League Division Two. In fact, they did better than challenge for it, because they won the whole thing. They didn't make it easy for themselves, though, as they had a player banned for almost the entire year for kicking a member of the opposition and swearing at the referee.

Cleveland League 1910/11 winner's medal
Courtesy of Kathy Martin

As well as continuing to produce world-class talent, teams in Redcar were putting the last few years of mediocrity behind them and once again competing alongside some of the best amateur teams the region had to offer. The town continued a long tradition of being founder members of important footballing institutions when several Redcar teams co-founded the Cleveland League, winning silverware on the first attempt. Their facilities were also garnering something of a reputation, with teams like Chelsea coming to train on their pitch before taking on Middlesbrough in the league. But things were about to get bigger for Redcar. Much, much bigger.

Chapter 6: Challenges

On Monday 5th May 1913, the town's football enthusiasts made their way to the Institute Hall to discuss bringing a standard of football to the town that hadn't been seen in decades. An idea had been mooted previously by Mr S. Williams, supported by James Howcroft and Harry Walker, about the prospect of forming a new club in Redcar that could challenge for competitions way beyond the quality of any of the town's current teams. At this meeting it was agreed: There will be a new team in Redcar, and they would challenge, finally, for the Northern League.

At a meeting of the Northern League on Saturday 14th June 1913, a decision was made about which teams would make the cut, with West Hartlepool, St Joseph's, Cargo Fleet Ironworks and Langley Park alongside Redcar as prospective new entrants. There were only 12 clubs in the league and none of them would be leaving, so the odds were stacked against all of them. But somehow, fate was on their side. The chairman Harry Walker, from Redcar, at the meeting, which was being held in Redcar, made a decision. For the 1913/14 season, there would be 13 members of the league, and the team that would be joining the current 12 would be Redcar.

Their first practice match was almost exactly two months later at Redcar Racecourse. Watched on by the manager of Middlesbrough FC, alongside two of their directors, Boro had promised to help all they could in helping Redcar become a success. "The committee were quite satisfied with the result," spoke The *Gazette* about the practice match, "and have little doubt as to their ability to get a team worthy of a Northern League club."[105] More than 70 players had applied to take part in trial matches for Redcar, so they had the benefit of selecting some of the best amateur players the region had to offer.

Redcar's home ground was to be at the racecourse, a venue that had hosted many important football fixtures over the years, home to Redcar and Coatham YMCA all the way back in 1878. The chairman of the Race Company was the Marquis of Zetland, who granted the new Redcar team use of a portion of the racecourse:

"The committee of the Redcar Football Club have selected as a playing pitch the portion of the racecourse between the main entrance and the stables, so that the ground will be only a few yards from the jockey boys' quarters which are to be used as the dressing rooms." [106]

As the new season began, after almost a quarter of a century of waiting, Redcar fans descended upon Redcar Racecourse to watch their team finally compete in the Northern League. Among them was Charles Skelton, a promising 18-year-old, and Harold Robinson, an impressive left winger who had signed from Stockton. A thousand people turned up to watch the match against Craghead, who were in their second and final season in the Northern League, seemingly fizzling out altogether in the 1920s. They were a decent side, though, and had finished a respectable fifth place the season before.

Redcar looked like the better team in the first half, with their best chance coming after 15 minutes, when Jephson somehow failed to convert a chance from three yards out. The teams went in level at half-time, but the second half was where Craghead showed their experience. "Although the Teessiders did most pressing in the first half, Craghead were the better side after the interval,"[107] wrote *The Yorkshire Post*, and it only took them 12 minutes to break the deadlock after the change of ends. They doubled their advantage shortly afterwards, with Craghead then being awarded a penalty shortly before full-time. However, although the game was lost, Billy Harrison - an FA Amateur Cup finalist with Eston United and younger brother of former Coatham United and Redcar Wednesday goalkeeper Harry Harrison - had a chance to show his ability, saving the penalty. The Redcar fans walked home disappointed, though, and that was to be a routine they would follow for a long time.

The 2-0 defeat to Craghead was followed by a loss against Northern League giants Crook Town. It was starting to become a familiar story; the first half was quite well-balanced, with Crook holding a narrow 1-0 lead at the interval. However, Redcar once again fell to pieces in the second half, allowing three more goals in. "Redcar have not been favoured with the best of luck since their inception," wrote the *Sports Gazette* after the Crook defeat. "Injuries have been received by several of the players, which probably means that for some weeks to come, the team will not be at full strength."[108] They weren't wrong.

The end of September saw Redcar back in a competition that, unlike the Northern League, the town was well-accustomed to: The FA Cup. It had been 24 years since Redcar's last engagement in the competition, the 3-0 loss to Clinton in the first qualifying round. Although it was no doubt good to be back, it would not be the reunion some may have hoped for. North Eastern League side Spennymoor were their opponents in a match played in front of 1,000 spectators in County Durham. Despite holding Spennymoor for some parts of the game, and Harrison who "saved splendidly on several occasions,"[109] it was an 8-2 demolition and Redcar were unceremoniously dumped out of the cup at the first attempt. "I'd 8-2 be a Redcar fan right now," the home support may have joked. As a strange quirk of fate, Billy Harrison's brother Harry played against Spennymoor in a league encounter for Middlesbrough Reserves just a few weeks later, making several smart saves and keeping a clean sheet in a 1-0 win.

This theme carried on month after month. "In the first half the home club did most of the pressing," wrote *The Yorkshire Post* of an FA Amateur Cup game against West

Hartlepool Expansion at Redcar Racecourse, but this game would end a little more controversially. Redcar won a penalty, which was subsequently converted, and West Hartlepool felt a little aggrieved. What followed were two red cards for the away side, one of them for hitting a Redcar player. Unbelievably, one of the players waltzed back onto the pitch and refused to leave, resulting in the referee abandoning the game. After an appeal with the FA, the win was awarded to Redcar and they had finally won their first game at home, although not in the way they wanted.

By November, Redcar were rooted to the bottom of the Northern League. They lost 1-0 to Grangetown thanks to a penalty, and an experiment to use left winger Harold Robinson as a centre forward that didn't pay off. However, tributes were paid to Billy Harrison's performance in goal and Bobbie Sturman's tireless performance as captain. "A draw would have been a true representation of the game,"[110] said the *Sports Gazette*.

Despite the positives threatening to make an impact on Redcar's woeful start to the season, it would get worse before it got better. "Poor Redcar!" wrote the *Sports Gazette* in mid-December. "Four Northern League matches played and all been lost; nine goals scored against them, and not one registered by the Recruits. What a tale of woe!"[111] It's true that it had been the worst possible start, but an earlier article in the publication had posited that it was not for lack of quality that Redcar languished at the foot of the table, but confidence. The longer they had to wait for a league goal, though, the more their confidence would be eaten away.

Enter Leadgate Park. Redcar travelled to County Durham just after Christmas, their opponents sitting comfortably in mid-table having just signed a new centre forward from Chesterfield. Redcar started the game in typical fashion, pressing their opponents and seeing large periods of superiority. Just before half-time, though, Young found Skelton who put the ball between the sticks to become the club's first ever Northern League goalscorer. As usual, though, they let their opponents back into the game in the second half, with "the Seasiders being rarely in the danger zone," according to the *Newcastle Daily Chronicle* report. The Highway to the Danger Zone was a road well-travelled for Redcar this season, and they walked that path again when they gave away another penalty. George Elliott scored for Park, and despite the kitchen sink being thrown at Billy Harrison in the Redcar goal in the closing stages, "their forwards seemed to be able to do almost everything but find the net."[112] The game finished 1-1 and Redcar - goalscorers at last - had another point.

It hadn't been an easy start to life in the Northern League for Redcar, but people were still remaining positive. Results were starting to come, the young and inexperienced team were starting to gel after multiple injury problems, and the cash was still coming in. However, as the New Year celebrations rolled on and Redcar welcomed 1914, gut-wrenching news was about to rock the club. Councillor Samuel Shewell, a popular figure who worked on the Urban Council alongside James Howcroft, passed away. Samuel was instrumental in the formation of the new Redcar club, acting as chairman of the committee, and his advice, generosity and deep wallet were a vital component in the club finally reaching the Northern League. Their struggles, however bad they had seemed before, now looked unsurmountable.

A few days later, Redcar organised a social night in order to raise funds for the club. It was a fairly big success. Over 350 people turned up to the Pier Pavilion which provided a much-needed injection of cash into the club. Back on the field, though, it was business as usual. January saw a 6-0 drubbing at the hands of Bishop Auckland and Redcar still didn't have a league win. The following week, The *Gazette* wrote: "Redcar will be lucky if their first League win comes at Stockton, as the Ancients don't give much away on their own ground."[113] Stockton won 5-3.

But then came Eston. Eston United were a very good team, and had won back-to-back Northern League titles in 1909/10 and 1910/11, reaching the FA Amateur Cup final twice in the past five seasons. So when Redcar came to visit at the end of January, everyone knew how the game would go. The teams took to the field, ready for kick off. Well, actually only one team did. Eston were still trying to scramble 11 men together. Time ticked on, and Redcar were still waiting. Then 15 minutes later, Eston emerged with 10 men. It was the best they could do. Despite their teething problems this season, Redcar weren't a bad side and with Eston's setback, they smelled blood. They immediately started bombarding Eston's goal, and Watson should have scored when he drove the ball high over the crossbar. However, after 20 minutes he made amends and put Redcar 1-0 up. Eston, with a mountain to climb, gave up. Watson scored again in the second half then made it a hat-trick late on (the first member of the club to do so), giving Redcar a historic 3-0 win. "Eston derived little satisfaction by the visit of Redcar," wrote the *Sports Gazette*, "who almost swept the ground from underneath the United's players."[114] Points - and luck - were finally going their way.

By February, Redcar's run of form saw them with three points, with Grangetown just above them. On paper the two teams were evenly matched, but when they faced each other, there was only one team in it. Although Grangetown managed to take the lead, Redcar were dominant for the whole game, and "were by far the superior team."[115] Dixon managed to equalise in the second half, with hat-trick hero from the Eston win Watson putting Redcar ahead. Captain Bobbie Sturman put the final nail in the coffin, the result being 3-1 to Redcar in a vital victory against the team directly ahead of them. Unbelievably, the few points they'd managed to accrue over the last couple of weeks meant that they were above Stanley in the table, sitting in 12th.

Next it was the turn of Harold Robinson's old club Stockton to visit the racecourse. Strong winds and relentless rain made matters difficult for players and fans alike. Playing through the downpour, the Stockton forwards "were out for goals" but Billy

Harrison "proved himself as agile as ever."[116] The strong breeze at the back of the Ancients proved too much for the Redcar defence to handle, though, and the score stood at 1-0 to Stockton at the interval. But Bobbie Sturman, buoyed by his contribution to Redcar's win over Grangetown, had other ideas. Evans brought the ball forward, outwitting his opponent when everyone in the ground thought his chance had gone, squaring the ball to the Redcar captain who "banged hard into the net...his success as a shooter was like a tonic to the crowd." There were no further changes to the scoreline and Redcar had picked up another impressive point.

●

A curiosity of Redcar's disappointing debut in the Northern League came in their cup engagements. Their North Riding Senior Cup campaign began back in October, before they had even scored a Northern League goal. Given their woeful form at the time, it was more than a little surprising to see them easily dismantle Brompton 6-1 in the first qualifying round. Convincing wins against Great Ayton and Stillington followed, alongside an impressive 2-0 win over Eston just weeks before their 3-0 victory against them in the league. A 1-0 win against Cargo Fleet - no thanks to an open goal miss - put them into the final.

It featured a familiar pairing. Two old foes from the very beginnings of football on Teesside were to meet again. For one last time, the North Riding Senior Cup final was Middlesbrough vs Redcar. In truth, the game was nothing like the battles of the 1880s, the game being "the poorest for years." Redcar were a different team, clearly, but Middlesbrough only entered their reserves in those days, their attention focused on the Football League and national cup competitions instead. An extra bit of spice was added to the occasion, though, by the fact that the two Harrison brothers would line up in goal for their respective teams.

Redcar's league form spoke volumes about the gulf in quality, and Harry Harrison's Middlesbrough Reserves could have hit double figures against Billy Harrison's Redcar. "As the Borough get a lot of support from Redcar, I suppose they didn't want to be too hard on the 'fishermen',"[117] wrote *The Green 'Un* after Middlesbrough's decisive 3-0 victory at Ayresome Park. "What a contrast to when Middlesbrough and Redcar in the old days of 30 years ago used to be so freely discussed before and after the events, the two teams at that period being as good as anything in the country," the article reminisced.

Despite another loss, it was a good reminder of the quality the Redcar team possessed, and of the potential they had for the future. Redcar's high turnover of personnel, always high on the agenda that season with at least 27 different players utilised, meant that they had to request special permission from the North Riding FA to produce two extra medals to give to important players in the squad, including their captain, that had assisted in their cup run but missed out on the final.

*Goalkeeping brothers Billy Harrison (left) and Harry Harrison
Sports Gazette, 23rd October 1920*

•

Although Redcar had enjoyed a decent cup run, the same old write-up appeared when they returned to Northern League duties. "At South Bank, Redcar, who cannot win at home, think they can reverse the result of their first meeting with the Bankers, but it will be a great surprise if they do."[118] They didn't. However, a draw with St Augustine's shortly afterwards brought them a much-needed point.

"Redcar are hopeful of registering their initial home success at the expense of Esh Winning, but they must find a way to the goal first,"[119] wrote the *Gazette*. And find a way to the goal they did. On 18th April 1914, the crowd at Redcar Racecourse finally saw the home team win a league encounter, coming away with a 3-0 victory. Spencelagh, who would go on to follow a grand Redcar footballing tradition of appearing for the North Riding representative side, opened the scoring, with new recruit David Parsons scoring from the penalty spot. Esh Winning had a penalty of their own, but once again Harrison "saved magnificently."[120] Charles Skelton broke away to put the game to bed for Redcar, the score being 3-0 at half-time, and remaining the same at full-time after a "spiritless" second half. A few days later they frustrated eventual champions Willington to a 1-0 win, despite playing with five reserves.

A star in Redcar's considerably improved front line was David Parsons, nicknamed Micky, who had signed for the Seasiders in January having most recently represented Eston United. His goal in the Esh Winning victory was eclipsed by a hat-trick in their final home encounter against Leadgate Park. But it was a case of too little, far too late for Redcar even as they romped to a 6-2 victory in their final home match of the season, the floodgates opening at exactly the wrong time. The win couldn't lift them above 12th place Grangetown Athletic and they finished their first season in the Northern League as wooden spoonists.

At the end of the season, the secretary of the Northern League, Mr H Grey, spoke at the annual meeting that the season "has been one more consistent than brilliant,"[121] which summed up Redcar's season. The consistency, unfortunately, being losing. However, feelings towards the club were positive. The secretary continued: "The newly formed club at Redcar was elected to membership for one year. For an entirely new organisation, surmounting many difficulties, they have had a fairly satisfactory season, and seek readmission." With Craghead resigning due to the financial toll the season took on the club, and the strange choice to have had 13 clubs compete this season, the bottom two teams – Redcar and Grangetown – were saved from expulsion despite Harrogate and Scarborough joining. In fact, Redcar had finished the season with a small profit, and things were looking very positive for the future.

Micky Parsons
Sports Gazette, 13th October 1923

Although Redcar were re-elected for the 1914/15 season, there was something much more important looming on the horizon. The Northern League meeting to elect teams for the upcoming season was held on Saturday 27th June 1914. The very next day, Archduke Franz Ferdinand and his wife were assassinated as they travelled through Sarajevo. This propelled major European powers into an armed conflict that would change the world forever. One month later, actions were put in motion that would see more than 70 million military personnel mobilised over four years in a conflict that would become known as The Great War. Redcar Racecourse gave up their land for the war effort and it was used as an airfield and army camp. Without a home and with much more important matters to contend with, Redcar ceased operations for the 1914/15 season.

Despite the approaching horrors, the Northern League went ahead without Redcar for the 1914/15 season. Crook won the title, but the following three Northern League seasons were not contested. There would be no football in Redcar for the next few years, with the Northern League not returning until the 1919/20 season. A new team, Redcar and Warrenby United, did crop up briefly in 1918 though, with goalkeeper Billy Harrison keeping up his match sharpness by featuring for them in the Eston District League.

The airfield at Redcar's home at the racecourse served as a flying school for new pilots, training some of the most successful aces of the War; Raymond Collishaw, the highest-scoring Royal Naval Air Service Ace, Victoria Cross recipient Richard Bell Davies and Amelia Earhart's mentor Oliver LeBoutillier were all stationed at Redcar at some point. As a German Zeppelin travelled over the town's other spiritual football home, Coatham Cricket Club, sportsmen and war hero Bruno de Roeper flew after it, even jettisoning his bombs into the sea to make his aircraft lighter.

Among the brave men and women who made the unimaginable decision to sacrifice everything to fight the encroaching tyranny was Harold William Robinson. Formerly of Stockton, he impressed in the trial games for Redcar at the start of the season and became a mainstay in the team thereafter. A Linthorpe lad just like the Pauls brothers from the 1880s, he was even educated at the same school. He had joined the Yorkshire Hussars when he was still a teenager, and was called upon to serve his country in France in April 1915. Shortly afterwards, he was transferred to the Essex Yeomanry, machine gun section. He briefly returned home in March 1916 to marry his sweetheart, Florence, in a ceremony in Linthorpe. The

Harold Robinson
Sports Picture Post, n.d. 1912

following year he left for foreign shores to fight again, this time for the 14th Battalion Yorkshire Regiment. Then, on 5th June 1917, Harold William Robinson was killed in action. He was 24. Harold is remembered at the Railway Dugouts Burial Ground in Ypres, Belgium, and you will find his name at Stockton Town Memorial.

•

On Thursday 17th April 1919, a meeting of the Redcar Football Club committee was held. Members discussed the current situation compared to when they ceased operations in 1914, shortly before the start of The Great War. They agreed that things had changed considerably for the better in the few short years they had been in abeyance, with the population of the town having greatly increased owing to, in part, advancements in the steelworks that had made nearby Middlesbrough a powerhouse in steel production. "With the industrial developments in the locality, many young men have found employment," said the *Sports Gazette*, "amongst them not a few who have proved their prowess on the football field and a larger number who are anxious to do so."[122] Interest in the game was increasing, too, especially since this was the first team that the town could really get behind since the original Redcar and Coatham from the 1880s, well out of many people's memory by this point. So "the few who [were] left of the old brigade were thus encouraged to endeavour to re-form the club."

Their first game back in the Northern League came against Stockton, and this time they had a point to prove. Redcar had strengthened well ahead of their return, not least with the inclusion of JR McCluskey who joined Micky Parsons up front. Parsons would go on to re-sign for Eston United the following season, having scored in the FA Amateur Cup final with them in 1913. After his second spell with Eston, he earned a place in the Hartlepools first team shortly afterwards, but not before he made 12 Football League appearances for Lincoln City in 1919. In 1921 he would echo the achievements of William Harrison by taking part in a North vs South trial match for a place in the England side. Of course, by the '20s this match only acted as a trial for the amateur team, but an impressive achievement nonetheless.

McCluskey showed the quality of player they'd invested in by doubling Redcar's lead in their opening game after Jones had put them ahead. Cook replied for Stockton, but an equaliser was out of their reach and The Seasiders came away with a well-deserved victory. Redcar meant business. Next they came up against Scarborough, and despite going in at half-time 2-1 down, they managed to turn the scores around in the second half and come away with a 3-2 victory. Their return to the Northern League had got off to a flyer and they were sitting in fourth place in the table with a 100% record.

Redcar's 1919/20 team that vanquished Stockton[3]
Sports Gazette, 6th September 1919

Later in the month they faced Grangetown St. Mary's. Four hundred people went along to watch the match, which was delayed considerably owing to the fact that the referee failed to make an appearance. They say the referee is best when you don't notice they're there, but that's taking it a bit too far. Eventually, a retired official had to take his place in the centre of the field. Redcar hit the crossbar in the first half but the teams went in at half-time with the score goalless. Despite being the better side for huge swathes of the game, Redcar had to settle for a point, with the match ending 1-1. It may have felt disappointing to not come away with a win, but since Redcar had to wait until after Christmas to register their first goal in their last Northern League campaign, going into 1914 with only two points, it was a decided improvement.

The following week, a "very small crowd of spectators"[123] visited Redcar Racecourse to see the match against Scarborough. The visitors had made six changes to the line-up that was defeated 6-0 by Bishop Auckland the previous week. Despite the wind aiding them in the first half, Redcar were hopeless in front of goal. They had enough chances, but the ball kept ending up closer to the horses' stables than the back of the net. Then, out of nowhere, a Redcar forward cut inside from the touchline and took a speculative shot at goal. The Scarborough keeper made a complete hash of it, and finally – somehow – Redcar had scored. They continued to batter the goal for the

---

[3] Top row (right to left): Mathers, Moore, Jones, McClusky, Harris. Bottom row: Spencelagh, Kelly, Parsons, Speck, Felton, Thompson.

remainder of the game, but to no avail. It didn't matter though, because the game ended 1-0 and Redcar's terrific start to the season continued.

A brief break for the FA Cup followed, when lowly Brotton were too strong for Redcar and came away 3-2 winners. This was a huge upset considering Redcar's strong side and their dominant start to the season. From there, things began to unravel. Maybe their heads dropped after an unexpected loss, maybe they'd exhausted themselves, or maybe the honeymoon period was over. But when they played Bishop Auckland in mid-October, they were humiliated 7-0, followed by a 3-2 loss against Darlington RA. The next result would be crucial.

When they found themselves 2-0 down against St Helens the following week, it looked like the rot was setting in. A rally in the second half, though, saw them turn it around completely to win the game 3-2. However, this late comeback wasn't going to start another run in form, with Grangetown St Mary's winning 2-0, followed by a losses against South Bank in December and a weakened Eston United side not long afterwards. Another loss to Darlington RA followed, with the game going ahead despite "parts of the ground being under water."[124]

It had really been a season of two halves so far for Redcar. "An erratic side," according to *The Sheffield Daily Telegraph*, they nonetheless had the quality to beat whoever was put in front of them. FA Amateur Cup 1911/12 finalists Eston United and Stockton both lost to Redcar at the racecourse, but a post-Christmas capitulation saw them languishing in mid-table. Redcar had also taken the curious decision to play one of their forwards, JR McCluskey, at centre back for most of the season. When Bradford City invited him for a trial (in the centre forward position) they figured it was probably for the best to be playing him up front.

A 3-1 loss against Willington in January – a home match played at Ayresome Park after Middlesbrough Reserves vs South Shields was postponed - was followed by a 4-2 loss to Crook a short while later, then a 0-0 draw against Stanley United the following week. Things weren't looking great. Redcar were desperate to push on and show some improvement on their last outing or they would risk another last place finish. On top of that, the town was still battling to keep up with the attendances of other more established sides in the league. The early days of local dominance in the 1880s were a distant memory, and the townsfolk needed to be convinced of a reason to come and support them or risk following their predecessors into the abyss. If they were doing badly, the battle was as good as lost. No crowds meant no money. No money meant no club.

Outside of league affairs, Redcar beat Derbyshire side Hathersage in the second round of the FA Amateur Cup, setting up a tie closer to home with County Durham's Stanley United. The two teams met on Valentine's Day, but Stanley were in no mood for romance. They trounced Redcar 5-0 on the way to the next round and Redcar were knocked out of the cup.

•

James Howcroft was in his mid-60s by 1919. His efforts in bringing north eastern football to national attention continued long after his playing days were over and by 1919, his efforts were rewarded when he was recognised for his tremendous work and elected as a vice president of the FA. "Much satisfaction is expressed in Cleveland at the tribute paid to Mr James Howcroft, of Redcar, in being selected as a vice president of the Football Association," wrote *The Leeds Mercury*. "In his day he was regarded as one of the finest amateur goalkeepers in the country."[125]

James Howcroft
The History of the Football Association.
Geoffrey Green, 1953

Mirroring the highlight in Howcroft's career, 1919/20 was arguably Redcar's footballing high point. They had managed to finish eighth in the Northern League alongside some of the biggest names in north eastern football. Four of their players were chosen for representative games, and their FA Amateur Cup third round appearance was the furthest a Redcar team had reached, "the last representatives of the County of Yorkshire in the competition."[126] But underneath the surface, as we saw with the original Redcar and Coatham side, there lurked some unpleasant truths. The club was still struggling to encourage a decent crowd, and with the exception of the 1,000 people who visited Ayresome Park for their "home" game against Willington, they weren't competing with their league compatriots. Rugby was taking off in Redcar and they had a team to be excited about, which would prove problematic in the years to come.

•

After beating Grangetown St Mary's 2-0 at the start of the 1920/21 season, Redcar's first true test came at the start of September when they visited South Bank at the famous Normanby Road ground. The Bankers had won the Northern League the previous season, coming second in the league but winning a play-off with the two other teams that had finished on the same number of points as them - Crook Town and Bishop Auckland. The *Gazette* said their game against Redcar was "one of the most interesting and exciting matches ever played on the South Bank ground."[127] Redcar took the lead but somehow in the dying minutes not only did South Bank manage to snatch an equaliser, they managed to find a winner too.

It was a disappointing loss considering they were so close to taking the points back to Redcar against the reigning champions, but nevertheless the season had started brightly. Two games against Scarborough would follow, with Redcar winning the first 1-0 thanks to a penalty, and the second 2-1. By the end of September, they sat joint first in the table alongside South Bank with three games won and one game lost. This was their first ever run of consecutive seasons in the Northern League, and their commendable eighth place finish the previous term had given them some momentum this time around.

Unfortunately, though, a month of good results was masking an insidious threat. Redcar were a very new team, and their opportunity to build support in the town was severely hindered thanks to the outbreak of war. Five years later they had done a good job of rebuilding a team that offered genuine fight in the Northern League, but their finances were "in anything but a healthy condition."[128] They had done well to cover short-term losses after their first chairman had sadly passed away only six months into their existence, but they needed stability. They held several fundraisers throughout the year, and their return fixture against South Bank was hoped to draw a big crowd, with the champions bringing with them the Northern League trophy to display at Redcar Racecourse for the day.

Despite this small windfall, crowds at Redcar remained poor. Horse racing was a popular pastime in the town, and so too cricket, both of which had roots in Redcar long before football. However, that year another club would form that would threaten to drive the final nail in the coffin of Redcar's Northern League team. In November 1920, Mr HL De Roper wrote to the *Gazette* suggesting that the town should form a rugby club. "I am only a temporary resident at Redcar," he wrote, "but I am sure a XV could be raised in the town if someone would take the matter in hand."[129] Redcar RUFC would play their first game almost exactly one year later, losing narrowly against West Hartlepool.

It's true that the end was nigh for Redcar, but it can't all be blamed on external problems. They had shown at the start of the season that they could take the game to any team in the division, and they had the quality to rack the points up. Sadly, their luck was running out on the field just as it had run out off it. They had lost to Bishop Auckland at the end of September, and although they "tried hard to score,"[130] they couldn't prevent a 4-0 loss. This was followed by the aforementioned return game against South Bank, where Redcar lost 4-1. Darlington RA were the next team to visit the racecourse, and on paper the two were evenly matched, finishing at ninth and 10th place in the league last season, just two points apart. Unfortunately, though, Darlington won the game 2-1 and Redcar were slipping down the table. By mid-October they had played more games than anyone else in the division but sat in seventh place out of 14 teams.

Their poor form continued with losses throughout October and November. Grangetown St Mary's then visited Redcar, who were also having a poor season, giving Redcar one of their best opportunities to turn their fortunes around. It didn't help matters then, when Grangetown went 2-0 up. Mercifully, though, a fog so thick enveloped the ground that the game was ended early by the referee. The game was ordered to be replayed, as was an earlier loss against Eston, and Redcar had another reprieve. A 5-2 loss to Stockton Town – who were challenging for the title – saw Redcar drop even further down the table, sitting 11th by mid-January. The trend would continue practically all season long.

Then came a game against Crook Town. Come the end of the season, Crook would be sitting in third place and were undeniably one of the strongest outfits in amateur football at this time, summed up by the fact that the County Durham side had just returned from their second tour to Barcelona, where former Crook man Jack Greenwell was turning them into European giants. On 3rd April 1921, Barcelona and Crook Town played a 1-1 draw. On 16th April 1921, it was Redcar's turn to have a go.

Both teams started brightly, but it was Crook who were first to break the deadlock after a scramble in front of the Redcar goal. From then on, Redcar were the better team. They should have equalised after Crook's goalkeeper fumbled the ball, then hit the crossbar shortly afterwards. Ten minutes after the restart they finally equalised thanks to a penalty from Lawrie Crown, a talented full back signed from the local leagues in Wearside whose season had been dampened by injury.

"The equaliser had infused a fresh interest into the game"[131] as both sides chased a winner. Skelton, a mainstay in the team since the very beginning, had some golden opportunities to snatch the game from Crook but blazed them over the bar. Two minutes from time, though, he picked up the ball from 25 yards out and hit a "grand shot" into the top corner to win the game for Redcar. Less than two weeks after Barcelona had failed to defeat Crook Town, Redcar had done what the Catalans couldn't.

Despite this impressive victory, and a win against Eston United, these would be the only victories they would see for the rest of the campaign. Darlington RA, who narrowly beat Redcar 2-1 earlier in the season, pummelled them 5-0. Tow Law beat them by the same scoreline, with Langley Park winning 4-0 as well. Of their 26 games, they not only lost 17 but failed to even score in 12 of them. By the end of the season, Redcar saw themselves in 13th place, above only Scarborough. What was worse was the ominous fact that they "were facing an anxious time over finances, with virtually no patronage at all."[132] After all, who would pay to watch a team in such freefall? To put things into perspective, that season's champions Bishop Auckland had also won the FA Amateur Cup, not to mention Crook Town's recent friendlies with Barcelona. Some early results seemed to suggest that Redcar could give some of the bigger teams a run for their money, but it was clear that they were worlds apart.

•

Coatham Church Lads' Brigade, 1920/21[4]
Sports Gazette, 23rd April 1921

Dozens of clubs now littered the town, keen to emulate the successes of the original team that were fast becoming a distant memory. One such team was Coatham Church Lads' Brigade. The team were far from the dizzying heights of the Northern League,

---

[4] Standing (left to right): Lt H Tate, J Hobbs, M Dowson, G Natrass, A Maddison.
Sitting: JW Tate, RL Agar, HC Eves.
Front row: C Bull, H Watson, A Bosomworth, A Robertson, C Robertson.

and competing in national competitions was a pipe dream, but the spirit of the 1878 Redcar and Coatham club was still with them. That's because their captain was Ralph Lancelot Agar, the youngest son of Bob Agar who had so ably served the club for so many years. Sadly, Ralph died 10 years later aged just 30, and was followed a matter of months by Bob himself.

There's also the small matter of the FA Cup third round. Redcar weren't there, obviously, but Newcastle were, and they had elected to stay and train in Redcar before their match against Everton, with the Coatham Hotel being their establishment of choice. However, after a shock 3-0 win for the Toffees, *The Athletic News* decided that somehow Redcar was partly to blame. "It is difficult to know what to say about Newcastle United without seeming unkind," they wrote. "Their special training at Redcar had not endowed them with fleetness."[133] Given the season that Redcar had in the Northern League, maybe there *was* something in the water.

•

Looking ahead to the 1921/22 season, things were positive. Redcar had retained the services of Charles Skelton, one of the few original members still in the squad, and had made up for the disappointment of losing JR McCluskey to Grangetown by replacing him with an impressive young forward called George Newton. They had also significantly strengthened the back line with a now fully-fit Lawrie Crown, returning from a nasty ankle break in January, this was his chance to showcase what he could do.

Reports in the press at the start of the 1921/22 season were looking good too. Ahead of their season opener at home to Crook Town, the *Sports Gazette* noted: "The home club opened in good style last season, and they were in great hopes of doing the same this year, though, needless to say, they do not anticipate a corresponding slump."[134] It had been only four months since Redcar's shock victory over Barcelona's equals, Crook Town. Needless to say, if Redcar were achieving results better than Barcelona then there was potential for this team to achieve great things.

They did not help themselves, though, by delaying kick-off by 15 minutes. Less than 10 minutes later when the game was finally underway, things got much worse. Lowther, one of Redcar's backs, picked up the ball and weakly passed back to the keeper when he should have cleared his lines, allowing Dent to nip in and put Crook ahead. With only 17 minutes gone, the rather aptly-named Crooks, a fine case of nominative determinism, cannoned the ball off the crossbar but pounced on the rebound to double their lead. Defensive improvement followed, but Redcar never looked like scoring and the match finished 2-0 to the visitors.

Games against South Bank and Cockfield, the latter being new entrants from the Barnard Castle and District League in their first ever home game at Hazel Grove, both produced losses with four goals conceded, but a break in Northern League action for the FA Cup presented Redcar with an opportunity to claw back some dignity. Coming up against Guisborough's Belmont Athletic, Lowther atoned for his mistake against Crook Town by opening the scoring. The lead was doubled in the second half and Redcar had their first win, clean sheet, and had another FA Cup game to look forward to.

Redcar's 1921/22 Northern League team[5]
Sports Gazette, 11th March 1922

Back in the Northern League, things weren't quite so rosy. On 17th September, just weeks into the new season, the *Sports Gazette* wrote an ominous report on their return fixture against Crook: "Redcar's troubles which so thoroughly weighed down the club last season were, evidently, not yet ended for they occupied a cold and pointless position at the foot of the table."[135] A goalless first half was a much more positive result for Redcar than for Crook, but the hosts – who were regularly garnering crowds upwards of 3,000 – were too strong in the second half. A 1-0 lead was doubled shortly afterwards, and although Redcar managed to reduce the deficit before full-time, the game finished 2-1 and they were still without a win – or even a draw – in the league.

Their opponents in the next round of the FA Cup were Loftus Albion, who had shown their pedigree in cup competitions by reaching the semi-finals of the FA Amateur Cup

---

[5] Back row (left to right): Hobson, Crown, Murray, Scotton, Woods, Lowther, Johnson, Creasor.
Front row: W Newton, G Newton, Bean, Forster, Skelton, Machin.

the previous season, demolishing King's Lynn 6-0, before beating Wycombe Wanderers 2-0 to set up a tie against eventual winners Bishop Auckland at South Bank, narrowly losing 2-1. "Although their splendid exhibitions had not met with just rewards," wrote the *Sports Gazette*, "they were still strong enough to be disquieting to the Seasiders whose weaknesses of last season had not yet been overcome."[136] Giving away goals from the Holy Trinity of set pieces; a corner, a free-kick and a penalty, Redcar were their own worst enemies against Albion, and Dye's fine shot which had initially put them on level terms with Loftus was their only saving grace, bowing out of the cup after a 4-1 defeat. This was to be the last FA Cup goal the town would see their team score in almost 100 years.

October saw them come up against Stanley United in the league, themselves in a difficult patch. Redcar, facing a bright sun, took just four minutes to open the scoring with CW Bean, a recent acquisition from Coatham Grammar School, tapping in from close range to mark the perfect start for his debut. A

CW Bean
Sports Gazette, 21st February 1920

nasty deflection put a Stanley player through on goal shortly before the interval, though, and the scores were level at half-time. The Hilltoppers came out swinging in the second half and took the lead 10 minutes later. Redcar knew that if they were going to pick up any points this season, this was going to be their opportunity to do it. And it was. Bean was the man to equalise and put the first point on the board for Redcar.

Unfortunately, it seemed like the club had learnt very little during its short time in the Northern League. They had still failed to nail down a consistent XI, a problem which mired their previous campaigns. "It is not that the club lacks talent," wrote the *Sports Gazette*, "the team includes many fine individualists, but constant changes have been responsible for lack of combination, and to this may be attributed their ill-success."[137]

By mid-November, Redcar had managed to pick up a total of three points courtesy of two more draws, with Scarborough being the only team beneath them in the table by virtue of having played four games fewer.

More personnel had been added in order to try and turn Redcar's fortunes around; with Hobson, a right back, and Davies, at inside right, joining the starting line-up. But it was CW Bean that was proving to be the best acquisition of the season for the Seasiders, becoming only the third player in the club's short history to score a hat-trick.

This was the point in Redcar's season where they had an opportunity to turn things around. It had happened in their previous campaigns and saved some of their seasons from going from bad to embarrassing. In the run up to their game against Langley Park, Redcar had no fixtures to fulfil so were feeling fresh and energetic. Two minutes into the game, though, and their energy counted for nothing. Langley went 1-0 up, and after a good chance wasted by Redcar, the hosts made it two. After the break, they went 3-0 up, with Scotton scoring a consolation goal for Redcar at the end of the game. Langley were having a poor season, and a win could have turned Redcar's season around. Instead, it only served to cause more damage.

Redcar may have been experiencing yet another torrid time in the Northern League, but their reserve team were having the opposite experience. Competing in the Teesside League, as so many Redcar clubs had before, they topped Division B with 10 wins out of 12, and were still undefeated by Christmas.

As 1922 came into focus, so too did a milestone in Redcar's footballing past. On New Year's Day 1922 Tim Williamson would celebrate 20 years at Middlesbrough. He would not have much cause to celebrate that month, though, as he caught influenza and lost his place in the starting line-up to Harry Harrison, who kept his place for the rest of the season. Williamson won the position back the following season, his final game coming in March 1923 against Cardiff at the age of 38. His record of oldest player to represent Middlesbrough would stand for 74 years until Bryan Robson broke it.

Redcar ended the year with a home match against Darlington RA, bearing more than a passing resemblance to their first Northern League season in still being winless and bottom of the league. They started brightly though, capitalising on the blinding sun that blazed into the eyes of the Railwaymen's back line, who were "playing the one-back game." Bean scored early on, but his effort was disallowed for offside. He found himself in front of goal shortly afterwards when George Newton ran past practically every player, but the shot was too high and the game remained goalless.

Blackett, Darlington's goalkeeper, was working miracles between the posts, keeping shots out even when "he was hammered by no fewer than four opponents."[138] Bean had another chance to break the deadlock, this time cannoning the ball off a defender. Despite Redcar's best efforts, it was goalless at half-time. The bombardment continued straight after the restart, though, this time Davis being the nearly man after his effort was put a foot wide of the mark. The goal finally came with Adams scoring "a swift, oblique shot" to finally put Redcar 1-0 up. They pushed for a second, with Crown equal to Darlington's attempts to level the score, and the final whistle sounded to mark Redcar's long overdue win.

A draw with Esh Winning threatened some kind of momentum, but there followed a disappointing 5-0 loss to an average Stockton team. A long absence from league duties gave Redcar a chance at coming into their game against Cockfield with fresh legs, but a 2-0 loss followed. Another goal from Bean against Eston couldn't prevent a 4-1 defeat at the end of January. A week off followed by a draw against Scarborough gave Redcar something of an advantage as the "wooden spoonists"[139] of the league then played each other.

"The Seasiders were in dire need of points" as they faced Langley Park, putting out their strongest team to face the club directly above them. A goalless first half was met with the deadlock being broken within a minute of the restart, Baker putting Redcar in front before coming agonisingly close to a second when his shot grazed the woodwork. "The result was in doubt until the final whistle", but Redcar held on for a vital two points[6].

NORTHERN FOOTBALL LEAGUE.

EXIT REDCAR, ENTER LOFTUS ALBION: A WELL-MERITED PROMOTION.

Sports Gazette, 3rd June 1922

Redcar's final match in the Northern League was against Bishop Auckland, holders of the FA Amateur Cup who had narrowly missed out on retaining their Northern League title after finishing second to South Bank. Charles Skelton, who featured in their first ever match against Craghead in 1913, also started this match. A typically poor attendance witnessed the match, a 1-0 defeat, and the Redcar committee knew that there were to be some difficult decisions to make.

---

[6] Three points for a win weren't introduced until 1981.

Redcar failed to even score in seven of their 13 home games. They finished rock bottom that season and bowed out of the Northern League for good, managing only eight wins in two years. Their poor finances had been high on the agenda ever since their chairman and key benefactor sadly passed away only months into Redcar's first season, and their battle for crowds became increasingly difficult after the rugby club piqued the local interest.

This was the end of the town's involvement in the Northern League for nearly a century, but it wasn't quite the end of the club. Their second team had been competing in the Teesside League Division B and came agonisingly close to winning it, with just one point separating the top three. It was decided to recommend all three teams for promotion, but Redcar - having withdrawn from the Northern League - instead elected to compete in the Cleveland League for the 1922/23 season, also allowing them to compete in the FA Amateur Cup.

	P.	W.	L.	D.	F.	A.	P.
S'ton Malleable	22	18	2	2	75	18	38
N'by Magnesite	22	18	3	1	97	18	37
Redcar Res.	22	17	2	3	83	25	37

Sports Gazette, 3rd May 1922

Redcar's Cleveland League campaign, buoyed by the assistance of their Northern League heroes Charles Skelton and Billy Harrison amongst many others, was so successful that they found themselves still unbeaten by mid-March. A top of the table clash against Carlin How followed, and "it was practically safe to say that the championship depended on the result."[140] No thanks to a nasty injury from Redcar's Baker, Carlin How won the game which put them in the driver's seat for the conclusion of the season.

Unfortunately, for reasons that were never made clear, Redcar failed to show up for their final league encounter. Had Carlin How lost their final match and Redcar defeated their would-be opponents Skelton, Redcar would have won the league. Instead, this was to be the last involvement of the club in footballing matters. They didn't return the following season, and the few players that remained at the club moved on.

Many of those players made a considerable step up, proving that despite their disappointing form in the Northern League, the team had undeniable quality. George Newton, a recruit for Redcar's final campaign in the Northern League, had an unsuccessful trial with Middlesbrough the following season. He was eventually picked up by Bradford City, who had only just dropped out of the top flight. He spent a season at Valley Parade, playing mainly in their reserve team in the Central League, despite scoring a "beautiful"[141] equaliser against Morecambe in a friendly in September. Just two months after signing, he fractured his collarbone in a match against Aston Villa, keeping him out of action for several weeks and "adding to the burden of the Bradford City club in a time of need."[142] He joined up with Division Three North outfit Durham City at the beginning of the 1923/24 campaign.

Newton wasn't alone in making the step up to the Football League from Redcar's defunct side. John Harris, "a fast and bustling type of attacker,"[143] signed for Wolverhampton Wanderers in the early 1920s after a spell with Eston United and 18 months as an amateur at Middlesbrough. He had to wait a year for his Football League debut, but he didn't disappoint when he was finally given his chance. He scored the only goal in a win over Derby County in January 1925 and went on to make eight appearances for the newly-promoted Division Two side.

John Harris
www.watfordfcarchive.co.uk

He signed for Watford ahead of the 1925/26 season on the recommendation of Wolves teammate Val Gregory, who had spent nine years with The Hornets. He scored five goals in 32 games at Vicarage Road, including three appearances in the FA Cup. Harris was transfer listed in 1926, but no-one met his valuation of £100 and he spent a season without a club to focus on his work outside of football. A move back to the North followed in 1927, and he appeared briefly for Darlington and Hartlepools before spending a season with Barrow, all three in the Football League Division Three North. He ended his career at Spennymoor United in 1931.

Lawrie Crown, "a tower of strength"[144] for Redcar's final Northern League season and one of their few bright lights, had shown he possessed quality far above than anyone else in the league. After joining the likes of William Harrison and Micky Parsons in the list of Redcar representatives in the North vs South game alongside future Corinthian, Northern Nomads and England Amateur goalkeeper and one-time Coatham resident HP Bell, he also played against Bell in a Corinthian vs Northern League XI match and captained the North Riding team, the first Redcar player to do so since William Harrison.

This was enough to convince Football League Division Two side South Shields to offer him his first professional contract after briefly signing amateur forms with Middlesbrough. The speedy wing back played 90 games at Horsley Hill, both on the left and right, despite a nasty knee injury truncating his time with The Mariners. His standout performances caught the attention of Newcastle United, and he signed for the Magpies in 1926 for £2,750. To put that sum into perspective, just 12 years previously it would have been the highest transfer fee in the world.

Bury came calling the following season, and a slightly smaller fee of £750 was enough to capture Crown's signature, who was nearly 30 by this point but still described as "one of the most stylish backs in the game"[145] after a stellar New Year's Eve performance against Arsenal in Division One. He joined Coventry City in 1928, then members of the Football League Division Three South. He spent three seasons at Highfield Road, totalling 117 appearances in which he was made club captain. He retired in 1931 after a successful professional career, returning to the Wearside shipyards he had started at before his playing days.

Lawrie Crown
Courtesy of P Joannou Archive

The conveyor belt of success at Redcar shows that, despite the disappointments the club suffered in their short existence, the quality of the squad could not be called into question. The fact that so many players made the step directly into professional football shows how close Redcar were compared to a Football League side, perhaps more so than any other time in their history since the leagues were formed. They may have unceremoniously bowed out of existence but, like the original team before them, they left a mark on the game as a whole.

•

Rising imposingly above the rows of terraced houses in Manchester's Moss Side sat Maine Road, home to Manchester City until 2003. On Monday 9th February 1925, just two years after construction, 5,000 people braved the driving rain to watch the second international trial match of the season. Much like the 1882 North vs South match in which William Harrison competed, England vs The Rest pitted the country's finest against each other to prove who was worthy to wear the three lions. Amongst them were Aston Villa's all-time top goalscorer Billy Walker, Sheffield Wednesday's all-time appearance maker and all-time top goalscorer Andrew Wilson, as well as future all-conquering Arsenal manager Tom Parker and one of Newcastle United's biggest club legends, Stan Seymour. As they made their way out onto the pitch through the downpour, barely visible through the rain were black armbands. They were for James Howcroft. Poetically, only a few short years after Redcar's Northern League hopes had died, so too did one of the last shining lights of the original Redcar and Coatham team from 1878.

James Howcroft
Sports Gazette, 14th February 1925

By the 1920s as he approached his 70s, Howcroft's health had been failing. The average life expectancy at that time was a little over 50, so reaching his age was not taken for granted. After the death of Alfred Davis, Howcroft was voted to step up from his north regional role in the FA Amateur Cup Committee to be appointed Chairman. However, he only managed to attend one meeting under that role before he "found it impossible to continue an active connection with the game."[146] He died in Redcar on 9th February 1925, aged 72. He was survived by his wife Rose Ann and his daughter Violet. "Football has lost another of its valued friends," wrote *The Athletic News* of his death. "He was a worker rather than a talker, and there are few legislators who have talked less and worked more."

Tributes poured in from his countless friends following his death. His longstanding colleague Harry Walker, at a meeting of the North Riding FA, said that the death of their old president was "football's loss."[147] William Gill, known to north eastern sports enthusiasts as *Sports Gazette* Editor Old Bird, emotionally shared stories of his old friend with whom he had spent so much time over the past 40 years. Remembering the days when the Cleveland FA would meet in a building over which they had to pass a metal grate at the entrance, he said "his invariable greeting to me was 'hello, got over it again?' This was a joke at my being so thin."[148] He then recalled "on another occasion when I turned up at a match smoking a big cigar he cried out 'hello, being [sic] at those coconut shies again?' He was a splendid brother, and his genial presence will be sorely missed from our midst."

At his interment, much like the England match in Manchester, the weather was poetically miserable. *The Athletic News* reported it to be "pitiless rain."[149] Amongst the attendees were the Mayor of Redcar, members of the Football Association including his old friend Harry Walker, colleagues from the North Riding FA, family and friends. There is no question that Howcroft's tireless work contributed a great deal to the fact that the Northern League was considered to be one of the strongest amateur organisations in the whole country, regularly producing winners of the FA Amateur Cup and future Football League sides.

The esteem in which Howcroft was held across the footballing world, given his intrinsic link not just to Teesside football but the game in Redcar itself, seems almost impossible to comprehend by modern-day fans. The idea that a man who spent his entire adult life working towards the betterment of the sport in the town could be collectively mourned from the very top of football's governing body down to the grassroots he so passionately fought for seems unbelievable today. But simply put, he had no equal. Not in his day, nor in ours. "No-one has done more for the advancement of local football"[150] than Howcroft, said the *Sports Gazette*.

•

The loss of Northern League football in Redcar presented an opportunity for other teams in the town to put a squad together and push on for success. Among them were Redcar Albion who were founded in 1928 to compete in the newly-formed Teesborough League, which consisted of no fewer than six other Redcar teams. Their red shirts and black shorts held more than a passing resemblance to Redcar teams of old, and although they would not win anything of note for 20 years, their achievements would be counted as some of the most impressive and best remembered.

Another new team were Redcar Borough, with one of their standout stars being a regally-named teenager called John Deacon. He and his brothers had moved to Darlington from Glasgow and had each found their own success; Dickie played for Wolves and West Ham before going on to Chelsea, and Jimmy scored 52 goals in 149 appearances for Wolves, later playing for Southend and Hartlepool. John was described as "a dapper outside right, quick moving and businesslike"[151] who had made his debut in the Northern League with Cockfield in his mid-teens. He then moved to

Redcar Borough to compete in the Teesside League and it didn't take long for him to start turning heads. He was invited to play a trial match for Liverpool at Oldham, where he ended up scoring the equaliser. This was enough to convince Liverpool to take him on and he signed a professional contract shortly afterwards.

Unfortunately, he couldn't live up to his brothers' form whilst on Merseyside and he played primarily in the Northern Midweek League for the reserve side, with an injury in the middle of the season preventing any likelihood of making the step up. *The Liverpool Echo* made a case for him to be promoted to the first team in March, but by April he had been transfer listed. West Ham, who still had his brother on their books, signed John just as Dickie was departing for Chelsea. His career with the Hammers didn't seem to last very much longer, though, and it would appear that he ended up in the North Eastern League for West Stanley.

John Deacon
Sports Gazette, 14th February 1921

Fred Hopkin
Sports Gazette, 3rd December 1921

Although his professional career was short-lived, Deacon's interest from top sides wasn't a fluke, with other big names taking an interest in Chris Old, Redcar Borough's goalkeeper, and Elliott, their forward, at the same time. A key reason that a Teesside League side were producing such talent was down to their trainer, Fred Hopkin, a Yorkshire lad who had signed for Manchester United from Darlington at the start of a successful playing career. He holds the dubious honour of causing the Red Devils to be fined because they were paying him above the maximum wage for the league, as well as being given an illegal portion of his own transfer fee. An outside left, he then signed for Liverpool where he played 360 times on the way to winning their third and fourth league titles in a side that was dubbed 'The Untouchables'. After ending his career back at Darlington, he came to Redcar to begin his coaching career before joining the staff at Leeds, going on to work as a physio.

Redcar Borough were an ambitious side. In a meeting in April 1933 they agreed to try and find themselves a new ground five minutes from the centre of town, in addition to putting in a request to use the Redcar's coat of arms on the club shirts. This was all for good reason, because Borough had ambitions to bring Northern League football back to Redcar after a nine-year hiatus. These hopes were dashed soon afterwards, though, when the town clerk wrote them a letter saying in addition to a centrally-located home ground, they would need adequate dressing rooms and – most importantly - plenty of spare cash. The first two points were possible, but the third, as the ill-fated Northern League team found out, was much more difficult. He pointed out that the lack of financial support was why Redcar had folded, and urged the whole affair to be reconsidered.

Chris Old
Sports Gazette, 16th December 1921

Ambitions dashed and key players taking their talents elsewhere, Borough's crash to reality would prove devastating. With talented goalkeeper Chris Old joining Grangetown St Mary's and other stars already departed, a matter of days before John Deacon made his debut for West Ham Redcar found themselves simply unable to put a team together. They resigned from the league shortly afterwards and bowed out of existence. Another One Bites the Dust.

Redcar Borough's story shows how fine the line was between success and failure in Teesside's amateur leagues, and how easy it was for clubs to disappear forever on their quest of reaching the holy land of the Northern League. Sadly it wasn't to be, but they weren't the last Redcar team to try – and fail – to bring Northern League football back to the town.

•

Disappointments and what-might-have-beens aside, there was still a lot to be positive about. In 1934 Redcar Albion, Redcar Celtic and Redcar Westfield all reached the quarter-finals of the Stead Cup, an annual local tournament organised to raise money for the Stead Memorial Hospital which was opened in the town in 1929, with Celtic going all the way to the final. The team, made up of the town's unemployed, were up against Marske Rovers. If Marske won, it was said before the game, it would be the first time the trophy would ever have been taken out of Redcar.

The final was played in front of 2,000 people at Redcar Racecourse and was a "stirring battle."[152] Celtic came out of the gates quickly and "at times threatened to overwhelm their opponents," having the better chances in the early stages, with former Redcar Borough man Powell opening the scoring for Redcar. If it wasn't for the heroics of the Marske goalkeeper, though, the game would have been done and dusted before the teams had gone in for their half-time oranges.

Maybe they thought the game was already won considering their dominant display in the first half, but Celtic took their foot off the pedal when the teams came back out. "Marske were improved, too, and were the dominant side for some time," wrote the *Gazette*. They capitalised on their ascendancy by equalising, and then a short time later taking the lead. Celtic finally found their fighting spirit in the closing stages of the game, an excellent ball from the left wing meeting Onions who cleverly netted the equaliser. Then came the finest moment of the game. In the dying minutes, Celtic's Batty picked up the ball almost from his own half and hit an audacious shot nearly half the length of the pitch which looped over the goalkeeper and into the net. It was a goal worthy of winning any match, and with it Redcar Celtic had won the Stead Cup.

Redcar Celtic, Stead Cup winners 1933/34
Evening Gazette, 5th May 1934

After the disaster of Redcar's short time in the Northern League, it was important for the town to show that not only could Redcar teams challenge for silverware but they could also produce talent that would turn heads at the country's biggest clubs. "There was no need to go to Scotland or any other country for footballers," said the Chairman of the Governors of the Stead Hospital after Redcar Celtic's win. "Some of the young players they had watched that evening ought to go far in the game." The fact that Liverpool were looking at Teesside League clubs for their young talent was testament to that.

There is one small extra note on this season. Perhaps of little interest when considering what else had been happening in Redcar at the time, but another team had appeared that, in retrospect, is worth mentioning. That team is Redcar Athletic. They are not related to the current club, but it's interesting to see the club's name stretch further back than anyone had realised. They are seen in March 1934 playing against Redcar Traders in Borough Park with a player called Pybus in goal. A few decades later, there would be another Pybus in goal for a Redcar team when Nev Pybus signed for Redcar Albion. Athletic didn't last very long, seen playing games against Parklands in Middlesbrough and the RAF in Thornaby, but never achieving much. Over half a century later, that all changed.

Cyril Baxter
Sports Gazette, 4th November 1933

The early 1930s was a strange time for football in Redcar. It had been a decade since Redcar's last Northern League appearance, and teams like Redcar Borough discovered for themselves just quite how hard it was to get back there. Teams were becoming accustomed to looking locally for success, with the likes of the Teesborough League and Stead Cup becoming new aspirations for the town's clubs. Redcar's good name wasn't quite limited to a small pocket of the North East, though, because in 1933 former Redcar Wesleyans player Cyril Baxter moved to Cairo, Egypt, and formed his own team which included six Greeks, three Italians, one Egyptian and himself. Despite national dominance being behind them, Redcar's influence now reached all the way to Africa. That being said, John Deacon's move to Liverpool proved that the path from local Teesside leagues to professional football was not cut off from the undeniable talent that made up those teams, so why couldn't others follow in his footsteps?

Chapter Seven: A New Era

As teams in Redcar began to secure more talented players, there began a battle for supremacy on a scale that the town had rarely seen before. One of the strongest teams emerging at this time was Redcar Westfield. Among the squad was George Coupland, a mainstay of the team who had been involved with the club from a young age. Coupland was a natural sportsman, also appearing for Redcar Works' cricket team, playing golf as a member of Warrenby Artisans and tennis at Dormanstown into his early 40s. He would go on to co-found the Teesside Footballers Veterans Association, which brought together ex-players from the area – including local legend Wilf Mannion - after their playing days were over.

Redcar Westfield, Teesborough League runners-up 1933/34[7]
Courtesy of Joyce Charlesworth

Coupland's Westfield had been Teesborough League runners-up in 1933/34 in which they were dubbed "giant killers"[153] despite having the youngest team in the league. This moniker was earned thanks to results like a 4-1 victory over South Bank

---

[7] Back row (left to right): Hailstone, Coupland, Nightingale, Lynn, Thomas, Lewis, Gough.
Front row: Winskill, Jackson, Kelly, Horner, Henderson, Semple, Turnbull (hon. secretary).

Corinthians, in which Coupland bagged a goal, as a measure of revenge for an 8-0 defeat the season before. Runners-up medals secured and victory in the Teesborough Bowl to add to their silverware, Westfield were looking to go one step further the following season. Coming up against a host of local sides such as Redcar Albion, Redcar Corporation and Stead Cup holders Redcar Celtic, Westfield had a chance to prove themselves as the strongest club in the town.

By November, that case was looking very strong. Having dispatched the reigning champions South Bank Rovers in a "battle royal"[154] in which they stopped their opponents scoring for the first time in over 18 months, Westfield found themselves top of the league, with their only defeat coming in the Teesborough Bowl. So when lowly Lazenby came along, no-one could have anticipated Westfield to be coming away with a loss. "A draw would have been a better result,"[155] said the *Sports Gazette* of Lazenby's unlikely - and lucky - victory, and things looked to be going from bad to worse the following week when they found themselves 2-0 down to Cleveland Works at half-time. "After the interval Westfield played like a team inspired," said the match report with Chick Henderson, who had been free-scoring the previous season, inspiring his side to another impressive win. Henderson hit a hat-trick in a devastating second half which resulted in a 6-2 victory, and "with his wonderful steadying influence was a great general...the Westfield revival was due in no small measure to this player alone."[156]

Sports Gazette, 3rd November 1934

There was more danger of dropped points in December during one of the many Redcar derbies on the calendar when Redcar Corporation, without a point in over a month, found themselves celebrating a last-gasp winner against Westfield, only for the referee to disallow it for offside and the points shared. "Westfield will not have many escapes like this,"[157] warned the match report. Another Redcar derby followed the week after, with Westfield coming away with a more convincing 2-0 win over Redcar Albion.

They remained unbeaten for the rest of the season, also winning a Challenge Cup semi-final on Christmas Day to set up a final against Teesborough Bowl winners South Bank Rovers. Westfield, with an unassailable lead at the top of the table, pulled off an impressive league and cup double after defeating Rovers in the final and finishing the season four points clear.

Redcar Westfield's triumphant 1935/36 team
Courtesy of Joyce Charlesworth

More success followed for Redcar Westfield when they capitalised on their dominance by winning no fewer than four trophies in the 1935/56 season. They beat Redcar Albion in an all-Redcar final in the Stead Cup, with victory also coming in the League Cup and Bowl. The league title, however, was a different challenge altogether.

George Coupland's Stead Cup medal, 1935/36
Courtesy of Joyce Charlesworth

After a winning streak at the end of 1935, Westfield were in a three-horse race with town rivals Redcar Albion and strong outfit South Bank West End. It looked like South Bank had clinched the title with just two games left to play, despite losing to Westfield in a top of the table clash. Westfield then dropped points against local rivals Warrenby, meaning all South Bank needed to do was beat Eston Athletic in their final game of the season. They didn't. Westfield won their last two games and against all odds pulled off a magnificent Teesborough League clean sweep, cementing themselves as the dominant team in the town. However, as they sat on top of the pile for another season, surrounded by trophies and medals, they would learn an important truth: Nothing gold can stay.

By the close of the 1930s, Redcar Westfield and Redcar Albion were both competing in the South Bank and District League. Westfield dropped out of the league by the 1939/40 season and their involvements on the local football scene ceased, limited to a few short but brilliant years where they could claim to be the best team in the town. There were many teams who disappeared at this point in time, and with good reason. After more than 20 years of peace, war had broken out once again. Amateur sport began to take a back seat to other more significant matters at hand, and many local footballers were sent to fight and would never return home. It's unsurprising, then, that the following few seasons were affected greatly by forces outside of their control, although many leagues did continue into 1940.

With most local leagues abandoned and fighting continuing across Europe, it was an unusual time for the footballing world. There were some talented footballers who were exempt from fighting for a whole host of reasons, mainly due to their jobs or health. So in lieu of leagues or competitions, many amateur teams in the area only played friendlies, with most of them in aid of good causes. In fact, it wasn't just local teams playing these matches, but army teams as well.

In September 1940, the Royal Artillery played at Borough Park against a South Staffordshire XI in aid of the Mayor of Redcar's Ambulance Fund. However, the RA had a couple of decent players on their side. Amongst them, Scottish international Gunner John Kelly of Celtic, Gunner Harry Ferrier who spent eight seasons in the top flight with Portsmouth after the war, former Arsenal, Middlesbrough and Newcastle outside right Sergeant Instructor Ralph Birkett, who was also capped for England, and Sheffield Wednesday's Lieutenant Brigadier Jackie Robinson, who scored three goals in four appearances for England. In excess of 2,000 people turned out to watch.

Ernie Tuckett
Courtesy of Gordon Wallis, margatefootballhistory.com

Another all-star game was set for December 1940 when Redcar Albion played an Army XI. One new recruit for Albion was a player who had returned home from service in 1940 by the name of Ernie Tuckett. Tuckett was born in Marske and joined Arsenal as an 18-year-old after scoring in Guisborough Brigantes' North Riding Junior Cup final loss, which convinced Scarborough to take the youngster on. After a brief spell with Arsenal's nursery club Margate he turned professional with The Gunners in their

1935/36 FA Cup winning season. His appearances were mostly limited to the London Midweek League with the reserves, though, despite scoring six goals in one match. He made only two first team appearances that season.

He moved to Bradford City at the start of 1937 in a swap deal with Laurie Scott, who would go on to make 115 League appearances for Arsenal where he won the First Division and the FA Cup, as well as 17 caps for England. Tuckett's time at Bradford wasn't quite as successful, scoring four goals in 13 league appearances in the Football League Division Three North, going on to join Fulham in Division Two.

Tuckett was a member of the Royal Air Force, and towards the end of 1940 he had an opportunity to return home to Teesside. Keen to keep his footballing skills sharp after the Football League had been abandoned, he decided to bring his talents to a local team, and he chose Redcar Albion. "With their inclusion of E Tuckett, the ex-Arsenal and Bradford City player, and the return of J Newton at centre forward, Redcar Albion hope to be at full strength,"[158] wrote the *Gazette* ahead of a Cleveland League encounter. Newton scored four and Tuckett added another in an 8-1 win over Boosbeck Swifts a couple of weeks later. The following week, former South Bank forward Russell joined the club.

Big names were appearing for the side in this extraordinary period for the Cleveland League, but a match had been organised which would bring even more talent to the area. Another Army XI were to play in the town, but instead of another armed forces side, this time they would be playing against Redcar Albion. Tuckett, Russell and Newton lined up for Albion, but there was some talent on display for the Army side as well. Alongside Blackpool's William Park – who would go on to play in the Football League for York City and Scarborough – was Spennymoor duo Penberthy and Gorman, Darlington's Dawson and Dover of Liverpool.

"It takes a long time to make a good footballer, and war is a more deadly game than football,"[159] wrote the *Gazette* at the end of December 1940. Although Ernie Tuckett had spent seven seasons on the books at Fulham, he only played one game for them – a 1-0 victory over Chesterfield in 1939. He instead concentrated on serving in the RAF for the succeeding years, and had risen to the rank of Corporal by 1945. Sadly, he was killed in an aircraft accident on 27th May 1945 whilst serving with the RAF Volunteer Reserve.[160]

Redcar Albion played another friendly later in the year, this time against the Green Howards. As time went on, it was more and more noteworthy that such matches were allowed to be played, despite the profits often going towards the war effort. Road signs in the town had been removed, the pier had been closed, and the sand dunes near the golf course were littered with landmines. Fear of invasion and attack was at the forefront of people's minds, and football was the last thing they were thinking about.

Redcar Westfield's George Coupland had ambitions to join Ernie Tuckett in the RAF, but was forced to join the Home Guard as a result of the knee injury that had ended his playing career. On 21st October 1941, he was part of the group that responded to one of the most infamous attacks on Redcar soil during World War II. Three bombs dropped on the town, one of which hitting the Zetland Club, killing the Mayor, as well as councillors and other prominent members of the town. Fifteen people lost their lives in the attack, with Coupland bravely attending to the scene to make sure that number didn't rise. He also manned one of the guns at the steelworks, which was a high priority target for the Luftwaffe. Ten people were killed at an attack on Warrenby Steelworks in November 1941, with more casualties in an attack two months later. The town is indebted to people like George Coupland and Ernie Tuckett, whose sacrifices ensured that the area didn't suffer more damage and that more lives were not lost.

•

Peter McWilliam
Sports Gazette, 8th January 1927

By 1942 there was some news at the very top of English football which had several connections to Redcar, but for context we must go back in time over half a century to 1889. Three years after Redcar famously made their way to the last eight of the FA Cup, the club was under the stewardship of messrs Woof and Coverdale. Their red and white stripes were the second set of colours the team had worn in a little over 10 years, and their first foray into league football with the North Eastern League was less than successful.

Mr John Woof - one of Redcar's two honourable secretaries - was a player himself, having the dubious honour of filling the shoes of one of the town's greatest shot-stoppers, the "prince of Northern goalkeepers" James Howcroft, although he was also known to play outfield. He ended up marrying and starting a family, one of his daughters being Florence Woof. Fast forward another few decades to 1927, and a Scotsman named Peter McWilliam was managing Middlesbrough. A Scottish international, he also played just under 200 games for

Newcastle United. Whilst at Boro he met Florence Woof and the two fell in love, buying a house in Redcar and getting married.

By 1938 McWilliam's reputation led him back to Tottenham Hotspur, where he had first cut his teeth in management. He was a hugely popular figure at White Hart Lane having won the FA Cup with them in 1921. He had won the Second Division title with them in his first spell as manager, and he returned to try and to the same in 1938 after they had faced another relegation setback. However, Florence's health while living in London forced their hand in 1942 and he tendered his resignation, the couple moving back to Redcar permanently. Florence lived almost another 30 years, passing away in 1970, but sadly Peter died in 1951 at the age of 72, and is buried in Kirkleatham Cemetery.

A year later came the death of another successful footballing name connected to Redcar. RG "Tim" Williamson is the only man that could have challenged James Howcroft as the best goalkeeper from the town. He is buried in Coatham Churchyard, the same place as his goalkeeping counterpart James Howcroft.

•

The Redcar Albion team presented with the trophies from their victorious 1946/47 season
Sports Gazette, 17th February 1948

By the 1946/47 season as the dust began to settle and football returned to normal, Redcar Albion had usurped Westfield and established themselves as the strongest outfit in the town. Aided by the likes of inside forward Ronnie Shaw, whose form would see him make more than 400 professional appearances for Torquay United, they went on to win both the Cleveland League championship and the Challenge Cup, as well as the OAP Charity Cup.

The following season would see Albion win another trophy, beating Lazenby 4-1 in the final of the Stead Cup, but it was Redcar Works' time to win the Cleveland League double. They finished the 1947/48 season with the Cleveland League trophy, the Challenge Cup (where they beat Albion in the final) and the Guisborough Priory Cup. Redcar Works had been around since the early 1930s and were now establishing themselves as a force to be reckoned with. In fact, one of their youth players would go right to the top.

Mike Collins in action for Redcar Boys Club
Sports Gazette, 24th February 1948

Ronald Michael "Mike" Collins had appeared for Redcar Boys Club in the 1947/48 season, and the team featured in the Gazette for their Teesside Hospital Cup game against Middlesbrough Boys in the February snow. The following season he represented Redcar Works' 14-16 team and also featured for Redcar Albion's junior side, but by 1951 he would make a much bigger step. At the age of 18, Collins followed in the footsteps of Howcroft, Woof, Harrison and Williamson when the young goalkeeper's form brought him to national attention, catching the eye of Chelsea Football Club and signing as a professional.

Sadly, Collins' Chelsea career never got going, finding himself as an understudy to Bill Robertson for the duration of his six-year stay at Stamford Bridge, before moving on to Watford. He made only one competitive first team appearance for The Blues, poetically against Middlesbrough at Ayresome Park. "Here's irony," wrote the *Daily Mirror* ahead of the game. "Middlesbrough paid £25,000 for two new players yesterday, and Chelsea bring in a young goalkeeper they picked up for nothing on Middlesbrough's doorstep!"[161] In front of "lots of his boyhood friends," Collins had a decent debut, "and played no small part in helping Chelsea to save a point"[162] as the much-changed side came from behind to rescue a 3-3 draw.

He also played in a friendly against QPR two days later, but that was as far as his contributions in West London went. He spent most of his time in the reserves who competed in the Metropolitan and District League. A match report from 1956, a dominant 7-0 win over Horsham, exemplified their quality:

"Not once, literally not once, was Chelsea's goalie Collins called upon to save a direct shot. All credit to Horsham in keeping the score down to seven, but they were like an inexperienced boxer, pinned against the ropes by a brutal opponent."[163]

He dropped down the Football League in 1957 to play for Watford as a part-timer to accommodate his career as a joiner, and he eventually managed to wrestle the starting spot from Scotsman Johnny Curran and made 43 Football League appearances, including three FA Cup games. He left Watford in 1959 and ended his career at nearby Folkestone Town.[164]

Another goalkeeper to make the step from Redcar to the Football League was Colin Tinsley. A regular in the Redcar Boys Club sides of the 1950s, he was an apprentice bricklayer when he signed a professional contract with Grimsby Town in 1954. A spell with Darlington followed where he helped them knock top-flight West Ham out of the League Cup and, in the same season, featured in their mammoth FA Cup battle against Hull City which was forced to four replays, the last one being at Middlesbrough's Ayresome Park.

Colin Tinsley in goal for Redcar Boys Club
Courtesy of Jimmy Douglas

Tinsley then signed for Exeter City, notably being switched to play on the left wing after dislocating his finger in a match against Workington. Far from hiding in the shadows, Tinsley popped up from a corner and nodded home the only goal of the game. The following season he signed for Luton Town where he was an understudy to former England international Ron Baynham, replacing him upon his retirement.

Tinsley then made 70 appearances for Kettering Town before returning to Luton on a short-term contract, his final appearance for the Hatters coming against Southend in 1967. He ended his career at Dunstable, going back to his old trade as a bricklayer and also working a tutor at Carillion's Craft Training Centre. He had a long professional career which included over 200 appearances in the Football League, but his achievements would be eclipsed by another Redcar Boys Club player.

Bobby Smith (far right) lining up for Redcar Boys Club, 1947/48
Courtesy of Jimmy Douglas

Bobby Smith went on to win it all. "I was playing on Redcar Racecourse, for Redcar Boys Club against Grangetown, when one of the lads said to me 'there's a Chelsea scout on the touchline watching you',"[165] he recalled in an article for *The Sunday People*. He disregarded it at first, thinking that Chelsea wouldn't be interested. And even if they were, like many local footballers his age, his aim was to play for Middlesbrough. But Chelsea's North East scout Tommy Robinson was watching Smith, and by half-time he had scored four goals. "He said to me 'Bobby, I'd like to see you come to Chelsea'." This was even more impressive considering he was playing out of position at the time. "I was a full back in the Redcar Boys team until, one day, our centre forward failed to turn up," he said.

A 15-year-old Smith went down to London to play for their junior side, living with his aunt in Fulham, but he struggled to settle at first. "I didn't like the traffic. I missed the open fields of the North Riding and the peace and quiet," he said. He decided that London life wasn't for him and he set off for home. When he arrived back in his hometown of Lingdale, his no-nonsense father – who had just come home from a day's work in the pit – wanted answers. "So you didn't like it," he said finally. "Well you've got to like it. You're going back down there at the end of the week and I'll be taking you. And this time, you'll stay." And stay he did.

Mike Collins (left) and Bobby Smith (right) with Chelsea manager Ted Drake at Stamford Bridge
Courtesy of Joyce Charlesworth

After a decent few seasons for The Blues alongside Mike Collins where he scored on his debut in the 1950/51 season at the age of 17 with a "cool head and a splendid shot,"[166] he had done enough to impress the powers that be at Tottenham in 1955. "They begged and prayed us to part with Smith," said Chelsea manager Ted Drake. "We did not want to stand in his way, especially as he had a chance of establishing himself at White Hart Lane." With echoes of Charles Pauls' contributions to Preston North End's 1889/90 title win, although Smith was part of the Chelsea side that had won the 1954/55 First Division title, he only made four appearances all season. Homesickness abated and with five seasons of playing centre forward in the top flight under his belt, Smith moved on.

After a transfer fee of around £18,000, he won the League and FA Cup double with Spurs in 1960/61, retaining the FA Cup the following season and scoring in both finals. They went on to win the 1963 Cup Winners' Cup, and he left White Hart Lane the following season and remains close to the very top of Tottenham's all-time goalscoring tally. He also won 15 England caps in which he managed to score 13 goals. Not bad for a Lingdale lad who grew up playing football in Redcar.

There are more stories of success from this era where local lads donned a Redcar shirt during an impressive professional playing career. Bernard Fleming played for Redcar Albion in the 1950s, joining Grimsby Town in 1957 and making 22 league appearances. He also played for Workington and Chester. Eddie Murphy (no, not that one) played for Blackburn Rovers in the '40s before making more than 200 appearances for Halifax Town, returning to Teesside at the end of his career to assist Redcar Albion as a permit player.

Redcar Crusaders, Middlesbrough and District League Champions 1954/55
Courtesy of Jimmy Douglas

During this period, although some teams did find success – Redcar Works won the Cleveland League in 1953, Redcar Boys Club won the Stead Cup amongst various other local trophies, and Redcar Crusaders won the Middlesbrough and District League in 1954/55 – they were littered across the decade and could not be compared to the national success that players like Bobby Smith had achieved. "It's been a long way from the Redcar Racecourse pitch to the England side and Wembley," said Smith.

Chapter Eight: Invincible

Jack Bolton was an inside right who was part of Redcar Albion's most memorable period in the late 1950s. Jack was a promising player, having been spotted by Billingham Synthonia as a 16-year-old playing for Smith's Dock. "*The Billingham Post* came out on the Friday and there was a write-up," Jack recounted in 2020. "It said 'although Smith's Dock lost 7-0 it was no reflection on Jack Bolton, Smith's Dock inside forward'. They said we hope to sign him on next season! I didn't know a word about it." When he joined up with his Synners teammates, there was a familiar face waiting for him. "I walk in the dressing room, who's there but Brian Clough! We both turned to each other and said 'what are you doing here?'" Jack and Cloughie knew each other from their school days, but the partnership didn't last long. Clough only played a handful of games for Billingham, and Jack was tired of being played out of position, so both moved on.

Bolton ended up joining Whitby Town from Wearside League side Trimdon Grange in 1954, but after returning from a period serving in the RAF for his National Service, he found that Whitby had brought in a group of Stockton players who had been left clubless when the team disbanded for the season. So by 1957, he made the decision to take a step down from the Northern League and join ambitious Teesside League side Redcar Albion. "There were some really good players," Jack said. "Really good Northern League players, never mind Teesside League."

*Jack Bolton
Courtesy of Jack and Gary Bolton*

Throughout their early history, Albion played their home matches at Borough Park, moving briefly to Green Lane after Redcar Rugby Club's Mackinlay Park was extended to allow for an additional field. 30 years after Redcar's Northern League team met their demise thanks to the town's support moving towards the rugby club, the teams under the two codes were finally standing side-by-side. Not only were the facilities better, but Albion were unable to charge an entry fee whilst playing at Borough Park, owing to the fact that it was simply an open field, so the move also matched Albion's ambitions.

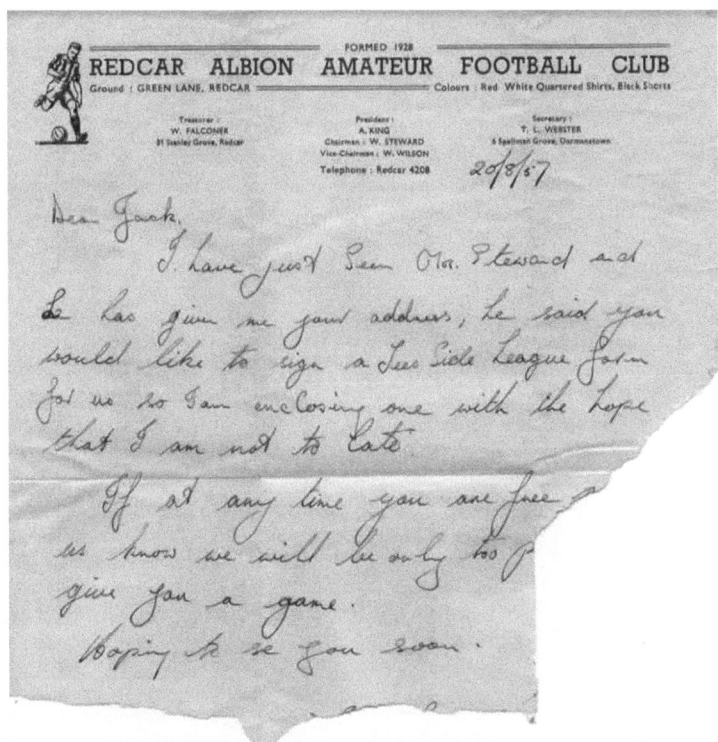

A letter to Jack Bolton inviting him to sign Teesside League forms for Redcar Albion in August 1957
Courtesy of Jack and Gary Bolton

Albion had shown some good pedigree through the 1950s; runners-up in the Teesside League in 1952/53, they then finished runners-up in the South Bank League two seasons later, but it was the 1956/57 campaign that showed that they really meant business. They won the Teesside League, the Ellis Cup and the South Bank League Challenge Cup, as well as finishing runners-up in the Priory Cup and semi-finalists in the North Riding Senior Cup.

On their books that season was a man who knew a thing or two about success. Tony Waiters, originally from Southport, found himself in the North East whilst on RAF service. After helping Abion win a host of silverware, the goalkeeper moved to Bishop Auckland in the Northern League before a long career in the Football League with

Macclesfield, Blackburn and Burnley. In 1964 he was given his highest honour, when the former Redcar Albion man was selected to play for England. He played five times for his country, and was also included in Alf Ramsey's initial 40-man squad for the 1966 World Cup, although he sadly didn't make the final 22.

Waiters finished his playing career in 1972, taking up coaching the same year and leading Plymouth Argyle to a Third Division championship in 1975. He then moved to Canada where he coached Vancouver Whitecaps to a 1979 NASL championship, followed by two stints as the Canadian national team manager.

•

With a strong team assembled, albeit without the services of Tony Waiters, Albion set out to defend their Teesside League title for the 1957/58 season. A 5-1 win over local rivals Wilton ICI was the perfect start, and it marked the beginning of a record-breaking winning streak. Bolton scored his first two goals in a 6-0 win over Head Wrightson, then helped himself to four in an 11-2 destruction of North Skelton. Not to be upstaged, his teammate Hill finished with five goals to his name. Both were on the scoresheet when Cargo Fleet were at the wrong end of a 10-0 scoreline, and again when the return fixture against Wilton ICI saw them win 9-1.

It was, in the end, all too easy for Albion and their team of Northern League veterans. Bolton's 19 goals from outside right was an impressive feat on his first season at the club, and helped Albion in not only retaining the Teesside League title, but breaking records in doing so. They won all 26 of their games, scoring a mammoth 127 goals and conceding just 18. Victory eluded them in the North Riding Amateur Cup and Ellis Cup finals, but success in the Teesside League Challenge Cup was more than enough cause for celebration as the season drew to a close.

But Albion's involvements in cup competitions were not just local. For the first time since Redcar's ill-fated Northern League team, the town finally had involvements in national competitions. The previous season, before Jack Bolton had left Whitby Town, Albion had come up against Whitby in the FA Amateur Cup, with another former Redcar player Nev Pybus in goal for The Blues. A 1-1 draw in the first leg saw a replay at Whitby the following week. The stakes were high, as the winner came up against Stockton Town who were on the brink of folding after rumours of the North Eastern League being on its last legs. "Because Stockton are not a strong side, despite the fact that they engage in a professional league, it would seem that Whitby or Redcar Albion will stand a good chance of entering the first round proper and thus qualify for the share bonus,"[167] said the matchday programme. It was not to be for Redcar, however, and it was Bolton's Whitby who progressed. They found it much harder than they expected against Stockton, who were fielding four ex-Whitby players, and could not overcome them. Stockton ended up reaching the quarter-final the following season, before briefly disbanding their senior side.

In Bolton's first season at Redcar Albion during their 'Invincibles' campaign, there was to be a replay of their run-in against Whitby in the FA Amateur Cup. As in the previous season, the first match ended a 1-1 draw which brought the replay to Whitby. This time, though, Redcar put up a fight. Their exploits through the season had seen them described as "the outstanding team outside the Northern League,"[168] and they showed exactly what they could do against Northern League opposition by winning the game 4-2. "I can vividly remember as we were coming off the field at the end of the match," recalled Jack, "the Whitby Captain Jackie May saying to me 'well done Jack, you were the best team'. You always find a good sport when you lose, not when you win."[169]

Their victory saw Durham City visit the town for the first time, whose formidable cup reputation was exemplified by the fact that they were preparing to host Tranmere Rovers in the second round proper of the FA Cup two weeks later. "We naturally hope that this is the only national competition in which they will make progress,"[170] said the programme notes. Sadly, Durham found more cup success and beat Albion 3-2 to reach the first round of the Amateur Cup.

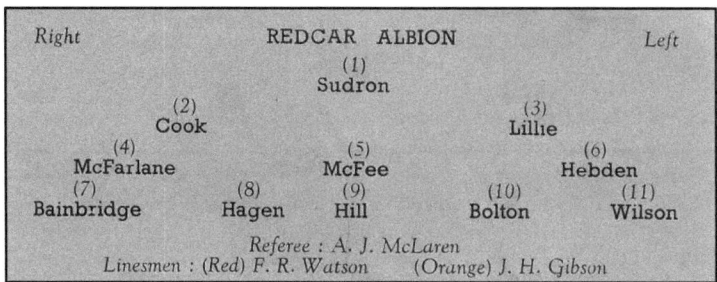

Redcar Albion vs Durham City FA Amateur Cup matchday programme, 23rd November 1957

They may have been known as the best team outside of the Northern League, but they were having trouble getting in, no matter how many times they knocked at the door. "Redcar always used to put in [for election] and maybe got two or three or four votes," Jack Bolton said, "but they were never really near enough to getting into the league simply because of the closed shop attitude." The summer before the 1956/57 season, six clubs – Penrith, Whitby, Stockton, Cockfield, Heaton Stannington and Redcar Albion – applied for election to the Northern League. But according to *The Penrith Observer*, "all except Penrith and Whitby are in a relatively small area and it will be against the avowed policy of the League if, by not re-electing the two present members, the area of activity of the league is narrowed."[171]

The league's "avowed policy" was adhered to and Whitby and Penrith – the bottom two clubs from the previous season – were re-elected. Cockfield, Redcar's opponents from the 1921/22 season, never again joined the Northern League. Nor did Stockton, who disbanded in 1975. Heaton Stannington, who left the league in 1952, would have to wait until 2013 to rejoin. Redcar Albion would keep trying.

•

Ahead of Redcar's triumphant 1957/58 season, and with Teesside League success in the bag from the previous campaign, they tried for re-election once again. At the Northern League meeting, held in Redcar, it was announced that the League's bottom two clubs – Tow Law, who tragically lost several of their players in a road crash, and, once again, Whitby – had been re-elected. Tow Law gained 13 votes, Whitby 12, Cockfield two, Esh Winning none and Redcar Albion three.

But Albion's chairman Bill Steward had a plan. "Look, this ground's coming up, we've been guaranteed it, we are going to build a ground near the fire station," he had told Jack Bolton. In a conversation with Redcar Council, a part of the playing fields on the Trunk Road had been earmarked for development of an enclosed stadium which would finally give the club a home of their own. Something of nomads, Albion had "been chased from pillar to post,"[172] playing in fields all over the town.

By 1958/59, Redcar Boys Club finished ninth in the South Bank and District League, with Redcar Crusaders immediately behind them in 10th, and Redcar Park Rangers finished third in the league's second division. The following season, Crusaders had slumped to 14th, with Redcar Boys Club in dead last, although Park Rangers' second place finish would see them promoted to the first division. These results played second fiddle, though, to what was happening at Redcar Albion by the 1959/60 season.

Albion's dominance in the Teesside League and plans for the future was a message that their time waiting in the shadows was over. There are many speculations as to why they were never accepted into the Northern League despite applying year after year, but by 1959/60 they had to take matters into their own hands. Exactly 70 years after Redcar and Coatham co-founded the first league by the name of the North Eastern League, who too had found themselves ostracised from the Northern League, Redcar Albion would join one by the same name.

Redcar and Coatham's first foray into league football was less than perfect, with only West Hartlepool finishing beneath them. But unlike the town's first team, Albion were on a hot streak and looked to be in the middle of their best form.

Redcar Albion 1959/60[8]
Evening Gazette, 30th April 1960

Although Albion were hoping to bring league success to the town that had been seven decades in the making, it is true that the North Eastern League was not the dominant competition in the late 1950s it once was. Football League sides once ran their reserve sides in the league, but many had left by the end of the 1950s. The remaining ambitious teams also departed, determined for quality opposition, leaving for the Northern League, Northern Alliance and even the Midland League. This didn't mean that winning would be easy, but it did present Redcar with one of their best chances to bring a slew of silverware to the town in years.

With that in mind, league success was not the only thing Albion were aiming for that season. They knocked two of the few reserve sides that were left in the league – Middlesbrough and Hartlepool – out of the League Cup, the latter 10-0, with Bolton helping himself to a brace. He was on the scoresheet in the next round as well, a 5-2 win over Wentworth, then scoring a hat-trick in the quarter-final against Bowburn. A 2-0 victory over Gateshead at Ayresome Park saw them meet South Shields Reserves at Sunderland's Roker Park in the final, setting up one of the biggest matches for the town in over 70 years. "When Redcar Albion, who broke many records in the local leagues, decided to join the North Eastern League, the critics said they had made a

---

[8] Back row (left to right): D Hebden, T Ruddy, H Armstrong, J Kelly, C Lillie.
Front row: J Bolton, J May, S Wilson, C McFarlane, J Morris, R Cooper.

mistake," wrote *The Journal* ahead of the game. "Against professional sides, the amateurs would not stand a chance. But Redcar Albion have proved them wrong."[173]

"Little Jackie Bolton, Redcar's inside right, was the chief danger man to Shields and was always there to grab anything that looked like a chance,"[174] wrote the *Gazette*. Although he was lively in the first half, neither team were able to break the deadlock and the half-time whistle blew with the score still at 0-0. Albion had plenty of attempts in the second half, which "were either too wide or saved by Shields' goalkeeper Anderson." Until Redcar's inside left McHale, who notched up 11 goals for the season, kicked the ball over his head to centre forward Jack May, also on 11 goals. May's volley across goal was timed to perfection, with Bolton – one of the smallest players on the field at 5ft 3in – heading in the opening goal after 77 minutes.

Redcar Albion blazer badge
Courtesy of Jack and Gary Bolton

That goal put Bolton on 11 goals for the season alongside May and McHale, putting them joint third in the goalscorers list, although none of them could touch Scott's tally of 30 goals, courtesy of three matches over the season in which he scored four goals. Redcar's lead was doubled after more good work from McHale on the left, who squared it for Ruddy to side-foot past the keeper in the 89th minute and sealing cup victory for Albion. They had no time to rest on their laurels, though, as there was still the small matter of the league.

Just a few short days later, Redcar faced Bowburn in the final league game of the season. Albion's league form mirrored their cup achievements, and they were sat at the very top. Their cup opponents South Shields were hot on their heels, as were Sunderland A, but Albion's slight points advantage meant that all they needed was a draw to bring a historic double to the town. The game would not start well. With echoes of Redcar and Coatham's ill-fated Cleveland Cup final match against Middlesbrough in 1885, when Bob Agar was so ill he couldn't put his own top on,

Redcar's outside right Ruddy, who had scored 14 goals in all competitions, picked up an injury.

Meanwhile, the teams in second and third place faced off against each other. Sunderland were on 30 points, one place behind Redcar on 32. They had to win if they had any chance of leapfrogging Albion to steal the title at the 11th hour, and after five minutes it looked like it could happen. Their early lead brought them level on points with Redcar, and now all they needed was for Albion to lose.

But losing wasn't something that they were making a habit of this season. They had only dropped points four times throughout the entire league campaign, with only two losses. And despite their disadvantage as "Ruddy limped on the right wing for most of the game,"[175] they went ahead after future Darlington player and Redcar councillor Stan Wilson opened the scoring. As Redcar grew into their game, South Shields were staging a comeback in their own encounter. Sowerby equalised from the penalty spot, and at the same time Jack May was taking the game by the scruff of the neck for Redcar. He hit a hat-trick to seal a thumping 4-0 win over Bowburn, with South Shields taking the runners-up spot after scoring a dramatic late winner. Albion had won the league and cup double, and now there was no-one who could deny that they were the best team outside of the Northern League.

Redcar Albion membership booklet 1963/64
Courtesy of Jimmy Douglas

But then another body blow came. Ready to mount a challenge to once again defend their title as they had so historically achieved in the Teesside League, they were met with the news that the North Eastern League would not continue for the 1960/61 season. Just as Redcar and Coatham's inaugural season in their league was not followed with a return, so too would Redcar Albion miss out.

With the demise of the North Eastern League, Redcar Albion's senior team went with it. Despite all of their successes, without a league – and continuing difficulties in securing a permanent home – they were stuck in limbo. Jack Bolton returned to Whitby Town, and their other star players dispersed around the area. Their junior side continued, though, and they would come to rely on some old friends for help. Middlesbrough, who had not been seen as Redcar's footballing rivals for seven decades, continued their tradition of lending a hand to their neighbours by adopting the team as their nursery club. They supplied strips and the occasional loan player and they would find some success during this time. The 1960/61 season saw them finish runners-up in the Middlesbrough and District Junior League, as well as finalists in the league cup and the North Riding Minor Cup. That season also saw Redcar Works win the Cleveland League – winning 20 of their 23 games and losing just once.

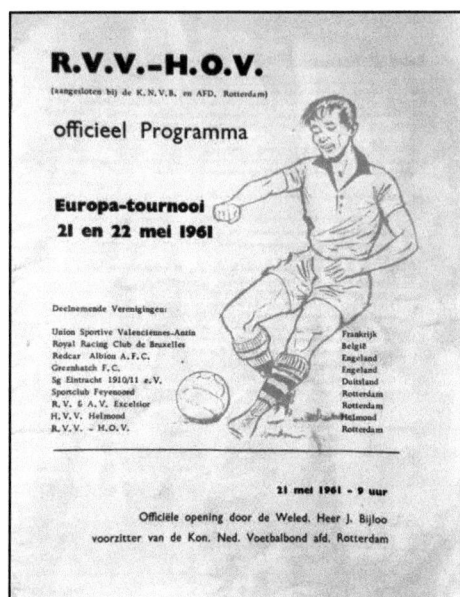

Rotterdam Youth Tournament programme, 1961

Albion's juniors then took their talents overseas against some strong opposition. In May 1961 they travelled to the Netherlands for the Rotterdam Youth Tournament, coming up against Feyenoord, Valenciennes and Excelsior. Many of these clubs had extremely strong youth sides, with academy graduates over the following few years including Kick van der Vall, who scored in the 1963 final against Ajax before playing just under 500 games in the Eredivisie, as well as Dutch internationals Hans Venneker, Wim Jansen, Johan Boskamp. Albion returned to the Netherlands the following season, coming up against the likes of Sunderland, Southend United and Eintracht Frankfurt. Although they didn't win, they still managed to see off some impressive opposition to reach the final.

•

Ahead of the 1962-63 season, the North Eastern League was reformed, having brought many of the old departed teams back. Redcar's return to the league did not echo the form they showed in their previous triumphant outing. Granted, it wasn't as bad as Redcar and Coatham's attempt in a league of a similar name in 1889, but by mid-February they had only won three of their 10 games, sitting 10th in the table. Their location in the league, though, was the least of their worries, because by 1963 they were more concerned about the location of the club itself.

Albion had always been nomads; bouncing around between parks and fields all around Redcar and Cleveland, but they had finally arranged for something they had lacked throughout their 35-year history: A permanent, personal home. It had been arranged with Redcar Urban Council, employer of so many Redcar players of the years, to secure a portion of the playing fields on the Trunk Road on which to build an enclosed stadium. Albion were in dire need of this; not only a fixed location they could call their own, but a residence from which they could begin to make money from their not insignificant attendances.

There was just one problem: The council were demanding an astronomical fee for Redcar to rent the proposed ground, and the club quite simply could not afford it. Jack Bolton had stepped away from the game by this point. "I was getting a bit old in '63," he joked. But that didn't mean he had walked away from Albion entirely. "I wonder if the Redcar Town Council realises the impossible task it has set the Redcar FC committee," he wrote in an impassioned letter to the *Gazette* that month. The total rent was around £660 a year, and Jack calculated that in order to break even they would need 440 paying spectators for every home game. "In these days of diminishing gates it may interest the Redcar Council to know that the average attendances at South Bank, Stockton and Billingham, all comparable teams, are around 300," he continued. "Even Middlesbrough Reserves can only command a gate of around 1,000."

He noted that fellow members of the North Eastern League were paying £70 - £100 rent, a fraction of the cost Redcar were being asked for. "The most outstanding example, however, is the case of Crook Town, the FA Amateur Cup holders, who pay a total of £330." The shocking statistic that Jack revealed is only made more ludicrous by the fact that Crook actually appealed that figure on account of it being too high. Redcar Albion were undoubtedly the best team the town had seen in living memory, and then some, but without the town on their side they were destined to lose. He ended with a summary that so easily could have been applied to Albion's forebears; Redcar and Coatham's ill-fated North Eastern League campaign, Redcar AFC's brief spell in the Northern League, and Redcar Borough's failure to reach it. "Every town on the north east coast and many villages...have senior league football teams. Why Redcar didn't appear to want one mystifies me."[176]

The club had already spent £1,000 that season in order to run, and would have had to have spent another £1,000 in order to complete their fixture obligations. In addition to the astronomical rent, Redcar Council had asked for a minimum of a five year lease, but due to unemployment and short-time working, the club did not want to ask for signatories to the lease and therefore wanted a yearly basis on the agreement.

Redcar resigned from the league in February 1963 and the club's record was expunged. Their record in the League Cup competition was three wins, two losses and five draws, with 18 goals scored and 33 against, their points total of eight seeing them sat in 10th place out of 13 teams. Without the senior side, all that was left was the team's juniors, playing on a workmen's ground. "The position of the senior side is in the lap of the gods," Albion chairman Bill Steward said. "We could not continue in the league with this uncertainty of a ground hanging over our heads." He said they would attempt to rent a field for the coming season, "but it won't be the same as if we had had our own ground, fenced in, and developed as a stadium. It is a great disappointment."

The demise of a Redcar team from a strong league was not a new situation in the town, and the latest addition came just over 40 years after the Northern League team resigned. Not only was the lack of support from the town a defining factor in both cases, but so too was the collective shift in interest towards the rugby club.

Somewhat poetically, Redcar Corporation's own team, competing in the Cleveland League in 1963/64, finished dead last. Albion's senior team did not run that season. As they found when they left the North Eastern League in 1960, submitting applications for new leagues was not always a straightforward process. They managed to win the South Bank League in 1964/65, but finished 11th the following season.

•

By the 1960s, Redcar had been generating talent that had reached the top of the game for almost 100 years; England internationals, Football League champions and unparalleled administrators. But when Alan Smith was signed to Middlesbrough's youth team he could not have imagined where his journey would take him. Smith had impressed in several school tournaments including winning the Redcar Schools Cup, where scouts from Raich Carter's Middlesbrough had been watching. "My dad knew and my mum knew but I didn't know they were watching me play for my school team," Smith recalled in 2021. He had done enough to earn an invitation to a trial, which was successful, and he was asked to sign schoolboy forms with them not long afterwards. "We used to train two nights a week at Ayresome Park, running around the track with one floodlight on," said Smith.

He played for Middlesbrough Juniors at their old training ground Hutton Road, which was briefly home to Redcar Albion after the club found themselves without a ground. "If we weren't selected for the junior team we'd play for the nursery team, in my case the nearest one was Redcar Albion," he said. "Clubs like Redcar Albion always had a connection with Middlesbrough." Smith was never allowed to realise his full potential, though, after a horrific injury in training ended his playing days for good. "I had a double fracture – fractured tibia and fibula at 17 which is a big injury, certainly in 1966." An ankle injury during recovery then set him back even further. "I fractured my right leg, dislocated my ankle on my right side, then I had my knee replacement at 65 years of age on the right knee. The left side isn't a problem!"

A Redcar Albion line-up featuring Alan Smith (front row, far left)
Courtesy of Colin Palmer

Whilst injured, Smith instead focused on obtaining his coaching badges, which brought him back to Redcar Albion. "I was able to get my coaching badge and coach the Redcar Albion junior team, that was enjoyable for me," Smith recalled of a successful, albeit brief, coaching career in which he won the North Riding Minor Cup with Albion.

Coaching aside, his recovery instead brought him a new passion: Physiotherapy. "It was Jimmy Headrige, the physio at Middlesbrough FC, that helped me recover from my injury and helped me towards a career in physiotherapy," Smith recalled. Headrige himself was forced to retire early due to a knee injury which prompted an interest in physiotherapy, and he encouraged Smith to take the same path after suffering a similar setback.

After completing his training, his first foray into physiotherapy was with Darlington, then being hired by Rotherham United in 1972, followed by six years at Blackpool. He then caught the eye of top flight Sheffield Wednesday in 1983 where he was involved in four cup finals. He may have thought he had made it to the very top, but there was more to come.

1984 saw him join up with Dave Sexton's England Under-21 side that were crowned winners of the UEFA European Under-21 Championship. Two years later, Sir Bobby Robson gave Smith the highest honour of being selected to join the England squad against Russia in Tbilisi. "Unbeknown to me I think they were looking at me," he pondered, "I think I was on trial." Much like his schoolboy trials with Middlesbrough, they were successful. After four more games with England in 1988, he was given the job full-time in 1994 by Terry Venables.

After representing his country at Euro '96 with Venables, World Cup '98 with Glenn Hoddle and Euro 2000 with Kevin Keegan, Smith retired from football after the 2002 World Cup Finals in Japan with Sven Goran Eriksson. "My last game was England Brazil in the quarter-final of the World Cup," he recounted. "Not a bad way to finish is it?"

After working in football for over three decades, including eight years working full-time with the national team, Smith retired from the game to set up his own private practice, safe in the knowledge that his achievements, which started out with the North Riding Minor Cup with Redcar Albion, had brought him to the top of the footballing world. "If you love the job, it's half the battle. You find a job you love, you'll never work again," he concluded, "I was like that for 32 years with football."

Chapter Nine: The Modern Age

On 1st August 1972, a stone's throw from Redcar Racecourse, two street teams formed by enterprising young men eager for a regular kickabout merged to create a new club. Both exclusively running junior sides, Newmarket Rovers and Epsom United – representing their eponymous roads on the Racecourse Estate – formed Newmarket United. The young men scoured the town for empty drinks bottles in order to raise money for their new kit, which was sky blue.

The 1972/73 season saw the club limited to friendlies, but the following season they became founder members of the Teesside Boys League, with Newmarket's first competitive game coming on 16th August 1973 against Yarm Wayfarers. Turning out in bright orange kits for the new season, the young men from Redcar showed their promise by winning the game 16-1 in a season that also saw them play in the TH Flory Trophy Final at South Bank's Paradise Field, narrowly losing 1-2 to Guisborough Town.

Newmarket United, late 1970s
Courtesy of Mal Bean

In the early 1970s, it would be easy to have dismissed Newmarket United as yet another local youth team of no real significance. But after several successful seasons in the newly-amalgamated Teesside Junior Alliance, including finishing runners-up in the top division, the decision was made to form a senior side, becoming the first team formed in Redcar that are still in existence today.

With echoes of Redcar Albion's trips to Holland in the '60s, a young Newmarket side embarked on their own European tour in 1975. Mal Bean, chairman and founder of the club, reminisced about their eventful trip in his book *When I Write My Book!* After arriving in France, it transpired that a game with the local schoolboys would be impossible as the French pupils were on their summer break and attending summer schools out of town.

After a discussion with the Mayor of the town via the hotel's owner, a match was arranged the following day at an old World War II army barracks set among the sand dunes. "What we saw suddenly took our breath away,"[177] Mal said in his book. "In the middle of the camp was a football pitch surrounded on all sides by embankments of sand dunes absolutely packed with kids all cheering, 'allez Calais!' as loud as they could." The atmosphere was unlike anything the young Teessiders had experienced in Borough Park or the streets of the Racecourse Estate back home.

The occasion got the better of the Redcar lads in the opening stages of the game, quickly falling 3-0 behind. The second half told a different story, though, with Mal bagging himself two goals to set up a tense finish. Despite Newmarket finishing the game the better team, the score remained 3-2, "but at least we had restored a bit of pride." They followed the match with an old tradition almost entirely lost to modern football as their hosts entertained them to a post-match meal. James Howcroft, way back in 1906, lamented the loss of this custom in an interview with a local newspaper: "The players took their opponents for tea, and then they all assembled for harmony. Such a spirit, however, is no longer a feature of our Saturday play."[178] Seven decades later, he would have been proud that Redcar teams were continuing to promote and nurture local football whilst still upholding its traditional values.

•

In 1978, 100 years after the first ball was kicked in the town, Redcar Albion had a celebration of their own. It marked 50 years since they were formed. 240 players and partners, past and present, attended the celebration at the York Hotel in Redcar. A few years earlier in 1974, the FA Council took the decision to abolish the distinction between professional and amateur footballers, simply referring to them all as 'players'. This meant that the England National Amateur Team – for whom former Redcar resident HP Bell played in goal several times – ceased to exist, and so too did one of the most prestigious tournaments for teams outside of the Football League: The FA Amateur Cup. Up to 100,000 people would watch the final when it eventually came to Wembley, with older finals being played at many familiar grounds in the

North East including Ayresome Park, Feethams, Linthorpe Road, Stockton and Bishop Auckland. The Northern League were dominant in the tournament, with no fewer than 20 finals being won by teams from the division. Redcar stalwart James Howcroft held the title of Chairman of the FA Amateur Cup Committee until his death. By 1974, though, the tournament was effectively replaced by a new one: The FA Vase. It wasn't a direct replacement, but the Vase was created in order to give the remaining amateur clubs a chance at silverware and a Wembley final.

Albion's first foray into the FA Vase came in 1979. At this point they were competing in the Teesside League against the likes of Marske United, Darlington RA and their town counterparts Redcar Works. Albion finished 11th that season, safely mid-table, but their first Vase journey would take them much further away than Teesside, with Carlisle Spartans being their opponents. This was actually Spartans' last season in the FA Vase, and possibly their last altogether, and although they put up a good fight Redcar managed to come away with a 2-1 victory. Redcar's first ever FA Vase campaign, despite indifferent league form, had started off well.

This brought them into the first round, and this time they would be at home. On their historic first ever home FA Vase match, they would be pitted against another Carlisle team, but this time it was against their bigger (albeit not their biggest) brothers, Carlisle City. The Northern Alliance side had knocked out Annfield Plain 5-1 in 1979 to set up the tie with Redcar Albion. Unfortunately, it was one Carlisle side too many for Redcar and they bowed out, 3-1 being the final score. Incidentally, Carlisle got knocked out in the next round by Smith's Dock, who won the Teesside League that season.

1980/81 season saw Redcar Albion once again win the Macmillan Bowl, beating Cassel Works 7-0. In the Vase, they came up against Boldon Community Association in what was only Redcar's second FA Vase home match. Their Wearside League opponents would finish 18th out of 20 teams that season, winning only eight games. However, despite Redcar's eventual seventh place finish in the Teesside League coupled with an Area CIU Cup and Macmillan Bowl double, Boldon were too strong for them. Despite a good turnout at Redcar's home ground at Borough Park, Boldon won the game 2-1. Redcar's home curse continued.

The next season, Redcar once again finished seventh in the Teesside League and once again won the Macmillan Bowl - winning 6-0 against Tees Company - and were sitting in fourth place by the time the FA Vase rolled back around. Their opponents in the preliminary round were Stockton Buffs, who were in the Northern Alliance, ending up in 14th place come the end of the season. A strong performance from the Albion side saw them come away with an impressive 3-0 victory away from home, teeing up a first round tie with Eppleton Colliery Welfare. "This should be a very entertaining game after our performance in the last round,"[179] said the notes in the matchday programme. Albion's team had changed considerably since their cup double the season before, adding a whole host of youngsters to the team. Unfortunately, their inexperience showed and Redcar lost yet another home Vase game, 2-1 being the final score.

The 1982/83 season would be Redcar Albion's last ever entry to the FA Vase. Their opponents were Peterlee Newtown, known subsequently as Peterlee Town. Peterlee were an established side, and this season they would win the Northern League Division Two at their first attempt, spending decades in the league's two divisions and regularly appearing in the FA Cup, taking Whitby Town to a fourth qualifying round replay, coming agonisingly close to a first round appearance. Sadly, this dominance was too much for Albion to overcome, and they lost another home game – 5-3 this time – on the way to Peterlee reaching the third round. That season Albion would finish twelfth in the Teesside League, but the following season did not make pretty reading.

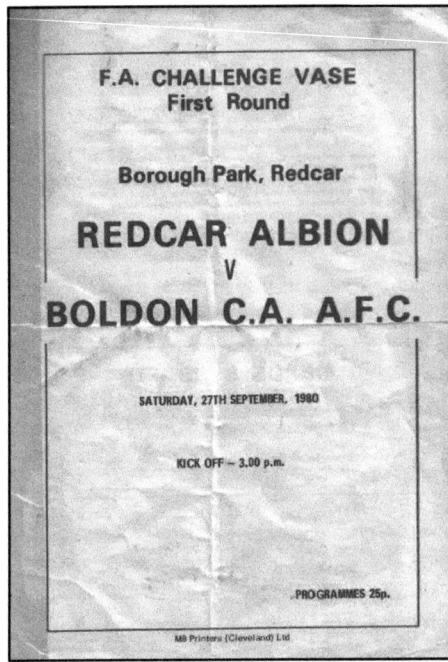

Redcar Albion vs Bolton CA, FA Vase matchday programme, 27th September 1980

They finished dead last in the 1983/84 season and did not enter the Vase. The final league standing saw them finish on 21 points, with just nine wins out of 34 and an astronomical goals conceded total of -103. By the end of the season, much like Redcar's Northern League side after their woeful campaign in 1921/22, Albion called it quits for good. Their 55 years in existence made them the second-longest running side in the town, behind Redcar Crusaders, but their glory days were well behind them.

Here we reach another point in Redcar's history where we can ask "what if?" What if the disagreement with the council had been avoided and Albion moved into their own purpose-built stadium on the Trunk Road? How could that have affected their standing in the North Eastern League? Could they have recaptured their form from a few years previously and won the title yet again? Could that extended spell of dominance have finally brought Redcar a place in the Northern League?

Sadly, once again, it was not to be. The 1983/84 season was Redcar Albion's last, and they bowed out of existence. Unlike the few seasons in the 1960s, they would not return. Alongside the woeful results from which the club could not escape, they found themselves hit with the curse that had spelt the demise of so many Redcar clubs before them: They had quite simply run out of cash. Redcar Boys Club, Crusaders and Park Rangers were still going, but one-by-one would also disappear. When the Boys Club was bought out by the council, the story goes that owner Mr Wright kept the memorabilia in a filing cabinet and instructed them not to touch it. Sadly, he returned to find the cabinet had been removed and its contents incinerated, destroying forever a huge part of Redcar history.

Meanwhile, Newmarket were continuing to build. They had joined the Redcar and District Sunday League in 1977, experiencing a glimpse of Redcar and Coatham's frustrations 100 years previously by reaching several North Riding Sunday Cup finals in the 1980s but "always seeming to lose out." They moved around Redcar in the years that followed, from Borough Park to Roseberry Square and Corporation Road, before settling at Rye Hills School – a specialist sports college – in 2004. They also saw several name changes during that period thanks to a number of sponsorship deals, but 2009 saw them officially become Redcar Newmarket Football Club as they made the step up to senior Saturday football for the first time. "That is the history so far," said Mal Bean. "We can only get bigger and better."

•

Teesside Athletic were a Middlesbrough-based junior side in the early 1990s, initially running two junior clubs. Their chairman, Alan Taylor, had ambitions to bring the side to Redcar and so began discussions with the local authority to make it a reality, where they were offered a site a literal stone's throw away from Redcar Albion's old stomping ground at Green Lane, just opposite Mackinlay Park. Re-founding as a Redcar-based football club in 1993, they increased to four junior teams including an under-7 side.

"My son was seven years old so I took him across," said Kev Fryett, who later took over from Taylor. "So then they asked me if I'd mind going on the committee and did I want to run the football team for my son. I said I'd help out until they find someone else, and they're still looking now!" It wasn't long before Teesside Athletic had 10 junior teams, and much like Redcar Newmarket, eventually decided that it could be time to form a senior side. "We realised the young players were going to come through the ranks and we needed somewhere for them to go and play," said Kev.

Like so many teams before them, they entered a team into the Teesside League, but their ambitions lay elsewhere. "We were always looking at trying to get into the Wearside League," Kev recalled. The caveat to their forward-thinking approach meant they needed to develop their ground in order to meet league criteria, which required the club to renovate their pitch - at the time a farmer's field - which was made successful thanks to a grant from the Football Foundation, which also helped to build new changing facilities and a lounge. "We were starting to become a proper football club then," Kev said.

With top of the range facilities secured and ambitions realised, Teesside Athletic embarked on their first season in the Wearside League - a feeder to the Northern League - in 2005/06 joining teams well known to former Redcar sides like Boldon CA and Jarrow. Despite an impressive fifth place finish in their first season, they weren't resting on their laurels. "We were always looking at going one step further and the Northern League was always our ambition, but it took us ages!" More ground renovations were required, but Teesside Athletic found themselves with far more obstacles to overcome.

From 2008/09 to 2017/18, they did not finish lower than fifth in the Wearside League, finding themselves runners-up on three occasions. "One year we finished second and they let the third team go up because they said their ground was in a better position for Northern League football," Kev recollected. But the team - who had changed their name to Redcar Athletic in 2010 to better represent the town they played in - continued working, on and off the pitch, and their efforts were finally rewarded in 2018 when they were promoted from the Wearside League as champions.

Redcar Athletic in Wearside League action in 2012

It had been 96 long years since Redcar had seen Northern League football, with many clubs losing their battle to reach those heights and going extinct trying. Redcar Athletic had nearly faltered on their own journey, but thanks to the resilience of people like Kev and the volunteers at the club, the town were able to celebrate much overdue Northern League status.

"Since then, everything's gone at a whirlwind really," said Kev. After a strong start to Northern League life with a seventh place finish in the league's second division, what happened next was something no-one could have expected. Two very strong campaigns were both curtailed by multiple lockdowns caused by the global spread of Covid-19, and for a time it seemed as though Redcar had suffered yet another devastating setback. However, after much deliberation it was decided to admit Redcar Athletic into the Northern League Division One based on their performances in the two truncated seasons, poetically making their debut in the league's top division on the 100th anniversary of Redcar AFC's final appearance.

Another milestone followed shortly afterwards when Athletic made their debut in a competition which had links to the town for almost 140 years: The FA Cup. It had been 62 years since a Redcar team had entered – Redcar Albion's 4-0 defeat away to Shildon. Albion's only other appearance the previous season was also away, this time a 3-0 loss to West Auckland, meaning that Athletic's home tie against Hemsworth Miners Welfare was the first FA Cup match in Redcar for just shy of 100 years.

Former Stokesley midfielder and Redcar captain Jordan Rivis was the man who had the honour of scoring the first FA Cup goal for a Redcar team in almost a century after Isaac Walker was brought down in the box, with Rivis slotting the resulting penalty away. Walker then helped himself to a brace after Hemsworth equalised, with substitute Owen Clarkson finishing a mazy run with a curling effort into the bottom corner to seal an emphatic 4-1 win on a historic afternoon in Redcar.

Isaac Walker was on the scoresheet again when Redcar faced Seaham Red Star in the next round, equalising after Seaham had taken the lead within the first half an hour. Despite Walker's contribution, their opponents took the lead again and it looked like Redcar's FA Cup journey had come to an end, were it not for a late red card for Seaham and an even later equaliser thanks to Bobby Rye, who tapped home from a Walker cross.

It wasn't to be in the replay, though, as Seaham progressed to the next round - and a match against nearby Marske United - courtesy of a 3-1 victory at Green Lane. Redcar may have been knocked out, but the sheer fact that the town had a team to support in the competition after the history they had shared in the previous 140 years was a much-needed victory for football in Redcar after so many setbacks. It may not have been a quarter-final appearance but for the first time in generations, residents of the town could experience what it was like to cheer on their team in the FA Cup, and celebrate a win.

•

In 1998, a team called Redcar Town joined the Wearside League Division Two, step 12 on the pyramid just below the Northern League. After a very respectable debut season in which they finished fourth, they were crowned champions the following year thanks to a superior goal difference over Stokesley Sports Club, with whom they finished on level points. Three seasons in the Wearside League Division One followed, including a fifth place finish in 2001/02 despite being deducted three points, but the following season they finished 16th, left the league and bowed out of existence.

Just over a decade later, a new Redcar Town formed. Taking on the town's coat of arms as their club crest, just as Redcar Albion had done, they started out life in the Teesside League Division Two. Both Redcar Town sides had come from the same club, a junior side which had been operating for decades, but the more recent iteration were determined to make a longer-lasting stamp on the local football scene. Winning a Teesside League title was something that the town was once very accustomed to, and Redcar Town brought back those memories when they won Division Two at the first attempt, also taking home the Macmillan Bowl, a trophy that Redcar Albion had won six times.

They found this success while under the stewardship of Roy Hunter, an ex-professional footballer from Saltburn who played for West Brom, Northampton Town and Oxford United. He had been convinced to take up a player-manager role for Redcar Athletic at the tail end of his career, also briefly playing for nearby Marske United in the Northern League.

Despite the similarities between Redcar Town and Redcar Albion, Town managed something that Albion struggled with so much over the years, and developed a ground on almost the exact spot that had been earmarked for Albion over half a century earlier. The council owned the land - as Albion knew all too well - but in the late '80s had tried to sell the area for housing, which is when a lawyer discovered a covenant on the land saying it had to be used for sports and recreation. "At the time we were nowhere near having a ground that was capable of passing the ground grading," then-secretary Derek Hartas recalled in 2021, "so we spent the following years doing it ourselves." Named after the town's much-loved former MP and Secretary of State for Northern Ireland, Mo Mowlam Memorial Park was built up to a high standard thanks to many volunteer hours and a bit of ingenuity.

Redcar Town's scoreboard at Mo Mowlam Memorial Park

"We built the dugouts ourselves, put the handrails round, bashed scaffold bars into the ground and we put the fence round," Derek recounted. They even used Roy Hunter's connections to obtain a piece of football history for the ground, when one of his former clubs Hucknall Town moved to a new facility, leaving behind the turnstiles that had originally come from Derby County's historic Baseball Ground which have found a new home in Redcar.

The team continued to push on in their division, with the exception of a brief dalliance with the Durham Alliance League, until 2017 when a mainstay of the local football landscape was finally laid to rest. Since 1891, the Teesside League had been home to a host of Redcar football teams and had been the source of some of the greatest celebrations and profound failures the town had witnessed on a football pitch. In fact, it had been the thread that connected the teams throughout the ages; from the fateful day that Redcar and Coatham withdrew from the league and disbanded, to Redcar Crusaders' questionable form at the turn of the century, Redcar Borough's struggles in the league after losing their top players to top teams, Redcar Albion's invincible years and the final season in 2016/17 where Redcar Town were joined by Redcar Newmarket.

Both Redcar teams joined the league that rose from its ashes, with the newly-formed North Riding League coming from the merger of the Teesside League with the Eskvale and Cleveland League. Redcar Town continued to build up the ground, sights firmly set on a familiar target. "The objective was to get them into the Northern League," said Derek, so the results of an advisory inspection of the ground was music to their ears: "They were absolutely delighted with our facilities." But ground grading was only half the battle. If they wanted to make it to a level that only two Redcar teams had reached in over 130 years of trying, they needed to show their quality on the pitch as well.

A third place finish in the league's inaugural season was the perfect start, followed by a sixth the following season and eighth the season after. Little did they know it, but the implications of the final table for the curtailed 2020/21 season would be more important than they could have imagined. Redcar Town were sitting joint-top, in second place thanks to an inferior goal difference to leaders Boro Rangers, when the Coronavirus pandemic put paid to the remainder of the season.

"I said if it goes all the way, football will change forever at this club," said Derek of the agonising wait to see if they had done enough to earn promotion. Then finally, they heard the news. Just seven years after their formation, they had achieved another feat that had eluded Redcar Albion despite years of trying. They were promoted to the Northern League. "Everybody's delighted," said Derek, "we've managed to get where we wanted to be."

In the end, the friendly rivalry between Redcar Athletic and Redcar Town had spurred each other on to greater success and had given the town something that it had never had before: Two teams in the Northern League. This was far from the ugly dealings of the failed merger between Redcar and Coatham and Redcar Crusaders all those years ago which had resulted in puerile arguments in the local press and infighting from which neither team recovered. Instead, both teams support and encourage each other, sharing a fanbase and working side-by-side to bring talented footballers to the town. The desire and ambition of both clubs has also resulted in unprecedented league success, impressive attendances and excellent facilities. Perhaps those old administrators bickering in the press were wrong after all, two teams can exist - and thrive – side-by-side.

Epilogue

The original Redcar and Coatham club had the world at their feet in the earliest days of football in the region; recruiting some of the finest players in the country and finding themselves at the forefront of the modernisation of football that laid the groundwork for the game we know today. They truly were pioneers. They entered the world in the days where games could be four sets of 20-minute quarters, the crossbar was some tape between two wooden poles and matches were randomly organised friendlies, punctuated by appearances in the earliest cup competitions. They bowed out of existence having helped to form what is now known as the North Riding FA, having competed in one of the world's first leagues and had representatives who went on to quite literally change the game.

Unfortunately, infighting and discontent snowballed from the controversial attempt to half-amalgamate with Redcar Crusaders, ongoing financial problems and the ever-increasing gap in quality between them and their oldest and fiercest rivals Middlesbrough, and not even a historic FA Cup quarter-final appearance could delay the inevitable and after several failed attempts at adapting to league football they threw in the towel, leaving the game in the region in so much of a stronger position than when they found it. With the tussles between Redcar and Middlesbrough being a catalyst for the rapid expansion of football in Teesside, every club in the area has Redcar to thank for the groundwork they helped to lay.

Although Crusaders were only a handful of years younger than their nearly-teammates, they found themselves in a similar position of struggling to improve on their form in the 1880s. They were mainstays in local leagues for decades, finally managing to compete on a national level as they entered the FA Amateur Cup for six seasons between 1896 and 1909. But that was as good as it got for Crusaders, despite being around for decades more and kickstarting the careers of future England players Tim Williamson and George Elliott, they remained in the local leagues until finally disbanding as the town's longest-running team.

Redcar AFC brought some pride back to the town after they gained the Northern League status that had eluded so many of their predecessors - and many of their successors too. But a devastating break after the outbreak of war spelt the end for the newly-formed side, who only managed a handful more seasons after breaking under the weight of financial troubles and loss of support. Their story is one shared by many teams that followed them.

Since then, Redcar Albion were one of the few teams to bring continued success to the town (with the very brief exception of Redcar Westfield) when their record-breaking achievements in the Teesside League saw them win the North Eastern

League after somehow still missing out on Northern League football. Ground trouble threatened the existence of the club, and whilst they held on for a few more decades, money trouble reared its ugly head once again and Redcar lost one of its favourite teams.

Despite a history spanning almost a century and a half, the story of football in Redcar has followed a pattern shared by so many teams in that time. Although Redcar and Coatham shared a heated rivalry with Middlesbrough, teams in the intervening years benefitted from a more civil arrangement. Redcar AFC were supported from the very beginning by the Boro committee, as were Redcar Albion who were adopted as one of their nursery teams.

This relationship carries through to present day, not only with the many youth products who go on to play for Middlesbrough such as former Redcar Athletic youngster David Wheater and ex-Redcar Town player Jordan Jones, but with senior players too. In 2021, just months after receiving the all-clear for his cancer treatment, former Ivory Coast international Sol Bamba announced he would represent Middlesbrough under-23s against Redcar Athletic in a friendly at Green Lane. In a move that was initially meant to help him return to match fitness, the game at Redcar kickstarted Bamba's recovery and he earned a place in the Middlesbrough squad for the following season.

Despite a healthy relationship with the town's more illustrious neighbours, a major problem faced by Redcar teams has been the battle to bring in, and maintain, a fanbase. While Redcar and Coatham battled Crusaders for superiority, subsequently falling behind to Middlesbrough, and Redcar AFC discovered an altogether new challenge when the rugby club was formed. Redcar Albion briefly attracted handsome crowds, but were unable to capitalise on the footfall while playing in open fields like Borough Park. Today, the two Northern League clubs are regularly attracting some of the largest attendances at their level across the entire country.

Now the town has teams competing in the Northern League and the FA Cup for the first time in 100 years, and after decades of waiting for a team they can get behind, there are now a handful that show not only quality but ambition. And maybe, just maybe, these teams have managed to break the cycle that had spelled the demise of the doomed clubs that came before them. Ali Brownlee, the legendary broadcaster known as "The Voice of Boro" once spoke about this ambition when Redcar Athletic were in the Wearside League and dreaming of promotion: "Hopefully one day Redcar as a senior team might make their way right through the divisions," he said of their Northern League ambitions, "who knows what the future may hold for Redcar? They might be pushing towards Middlesbrough one day. Who knows?"

Select details

Redcar and Coatham Football Club

These details are taken from CA Alcock's *Football Annual*. Honourable secretaries were encouraged to send in information from the previous season for publication, and as such there may be errors.

1879/80

Ground	Change	Secretary	Strip
Redcar Racecourse	Red Lion Hotel	James Howcroft	Black and red stripes

Played	Won	Drawn	Lost	Goals for	Goals against
9	4	3	2	13	8

1880/81

Ground	Change	Secretary	Strip
Cricket Ground	At ground	James Howcroft	Black and red stripes

Played	Won	Drawn	Lost	Goals for	Goals against
11	8	0	3	40	12

1881/82

Ground	Change	Secretary	Strip
Cricket Ground	At ground	T. Tutin	Black and red stripes

Played	Won	Drawn	Lost	Goals for	Goals against
20	16	1	3	68	21

1882/83

Ground	Change	Secretary	Strip
Cricket Ground	At ground	George Abbey	Black and red stripes

Played	Won	Drawn	Lost	Goals for	Goals against
17	11	1	5	53	27

1883/84

Ground	Change	Secretary	Strip
Cricket Ground	At ground	J.S. Pounder	Black and red stripes

Played	Won	Drawn	Lost	Goals for	Goals against
20	13	1	6	53	27

1884/85

Ground	Change	Secretary	Strip
Cricket Ground	At ground	E.T. Umpleby	Black and red stripes

Played	Won	Drawn	Lost	Goals for	Goals against
25	18	2	5	71	2

Note that the 'goals against' is incorrect, but the information was printed this way in the Football Annual.

1885/86

Ground	Change	Secretary	Strip
Cricket Ground	Lobster Hotel	John Bulman	Black and red stripes

Played	Won	Drawn	Lost	Goals for	Goals against
20	9	6	5	47	27

1886/87

Ground	Change	Secretary	Strip
Cricket Ground	At ground	John Bulman	Black and red stripes

Played	Won	Drawn	Lost	Goals for	Goals against
18	10	1	7	62	50

1887/88 missing

1888/89

Ground	Change	Secretary	Strip
Cricket Ground	At ground	A. Coverdale	White and red stripes

Played	Won	Drawn	Lost	Goals for	Goals against
29	20	1	8	90	40

1889/90

Ground	Change	Secretary	Strip
Cricket Ground	At ground	J.S. Pounder	Black and red stripes

Played	Won	Drawn	Lost	Goals for	Goals against[180]
13	2	2	9	21	32

Redcar Albion honours
1945-1967[181]

1945-46	Stead Cup winners
1946-47	Cleveland League winners
	Cleveland League Challenge Cup winners
	O.A.P. Charity Cup winners
1947-48	Stead Cup winners
	Cleveland League Challenge Cup runners-up
1948-49	Ellis Cup runners-up
	Stead Cup winners
1949-50	Teesside League Challenge Cup winners
	South Bank League Challenge Cup winners
	Ellis Cup winners
	Priory Cup runners-up
1950-51	North Riding Amateur Cup runners-up
	North Riding Senior Cup semi-finalists
1951-52	Ellis Cup runners-up
	Stead Cup winners
1952-53	Teesside League Challenge Cup winners (forfeited on protest)
	Teesside League runners-up
1953-54	Teesside League Challenge Cup runners-up
1955-56	Ellis Cup winners

	South Bank League runners-up
	South Bank League Challenge Cup runners-up
1956-57	Teesside League winners
	Ellis Cup winners
	South Bank League Challenge Cup winners
	Priory Cup runners-up
	North Riding Senior Cup semi-finalists
1957-58	Teesside League winners
	Teesside League Challenge Cup winners
	North Riding Amateur Cup runners-up
	Ellis Cup runners-up
1958-59	Teesside League winners
	Teesside League Challenge Cup winners
1959-60	North Eastern League winners
	Teesside League Challenge Cup winners
1960-61	Middlesbrough and District Junior League runners-up
	Middlesbrough and District Junior League Cup runners-up
	North Riding Minor Cup runners-up
	Dutch Youth Tournament runners-up
1961-62	Middlesbrough and District Junior League winners
	Middlesbrough and District Junior League Cup runners-up
1964-65	South Bank League Division Two winners
	South Bank League Challenge Cup semi-finalists
1966-67	Teesside League Challenge Cup runners-up

Acknowledgements

For a solo project, this has been something of a gigantic collaborative effort.

From the early conception as an article in Redcar's matchday programme, all the way to printing this book, I am indebted to the help and support of an enormous amount of people along the way.

My thanks firstly must go to Kev at Redcar Athletic and James at FootiePrint whose constant support and enthusiasm since the very beginning of this project has spurred me on, even when times were tough. Thanks for the encouragement.

Thanks also to the people who first laid the foundations of my research; Steve Roberts, who not only provided me with a wealth of resources, context and contacts, but also kindly listened to every minute update I gave whenever I found out any worthwhile information. Similarly, I am equally indebted to Gary Bolton, who not only provided me with the same support but also put me in contact with his father Jack, to whom I am incredibly grateful for giving up hours of his time to share his memories with me from his playing days. Thank you Jack, and no you weren't boring me! Similarly, thank you to Alan Smith for giving up your time to speak to me on your lunch break and digging out your own scrapbook in preparation, and to Derek Hartas for the invaluable information and for so kindly extending an open invitation at Redcar Town.

I am also very grateful to the many club historians who kindly allowed me to piggyback on their incomparable research to shine a light on my own area of interest while expecting nothing in return. Thanks to Tosh Warwick and Richard Piers Rayner at Middlesbrough FC, Paul Joannou at Newcastle United, Peter Law at Sheffield Wednesday and Ian Rigby at Preston North End. On the subject of historians, I am honoured to have shared in some research with the unparalleled Martin Westby and to have shared some fascinating photos (which feature in this book) before his untimely passing.

I must also thank the many institutions without which I would have very little information to go on. The British Library has been a haven for me throughout this period, and has provided me with resources that would otherwise be impossible to obtain. The British Newspaper Archive is another incredible resource, and thanks to Middlesbrough Reference Library, Teesside Archives, Darlington Library and Sheffield City Archives. Also thanks to Football Club History Database, EnglandFootballOnline, The English National Football Archive and NonLeagueMatters.

To the innumerable people who have offered stories, images, suggestions, contacts, links, articles and memorabilia on social media I am also hugely grateful. Namely the fine people at Redcar Memories, The Mighty Redcar, South Bank Born and Bred, Slaggy Island Memories, 100 Years of Dormanstown Celebration and Football Historians Research Group.

Thank you also to the people who kindly shared memories of their family members and allowed me to write about them. Namely to Joyce Charlesworth, present at many fine barbecues in my youth and wife to my much-loved scoutmaster Alan, who shared so much about her father George Coupland and his wonderful achievements. Thanks also to Edzard Pauls, the grandson of Edward Pauls who played football for Redcar's first football team, it has been a privilege to share stories about your wonderful family. Likewise Bob Newell, thank you for sharing your stories about Jacob and his remarkable achievements off the field.

I'm also indebted to my friends who kindly allowed me to make the most of their areas of expertise; Steven Renney who designed the beautiful cover, Mike Philo who wrote the excellent blurb, Andrew Easby who helped make sense of all the numbers, and Domo Smith, Jonny Whitlam and Mike Bloom for generally putting up with my ramblings and supporting me nonetheless.

I'm inevitably going to forget someone, so I apologise if I miss you out, but thank you to Margaret Daniel, Clive Nicholson, Mike Amos, Kathy Martin, Ann Rudd, Jimmy Douglas, Colin Palmer, Peter Holme and Wiebke Cullen, Adelaide Crapsey, Mal Bean, Bethan Jones, Neil Fissler, Phil Carter, Nick Catley, David Pallister, Shaun Wilson, Rob Cavallini, Philip Martin, Dominic Bliss, Fun Time Mikey, Dave Masterman, Pat Webster, Brian Milburn, Dave Lawrence, Derek Ditchburn, Bri McNeil, Stephen Dixon and Neil Harris for their help along the way.

Thanks to my grandparents for their genealogical research help and their fine advice in publishing books, and to my wife Kim and children Isla and Milo for giving me the time to do this when I probably should have been cleaning the kitchen instead.

Lastly, to my mum, who gave me a love of history, and my dad, who gave me a love of football.

References

[1] The Athletic News, 2nd October 1911
[2] The Victorians and Sport by Mike Huggins
[3] Redcar and Saltburn by the Sea Gazette, 18th October 1878
[4] The Athletic News, 2nd October 1911
[5] Stockton Herald, South Durham and Cleveland Advertiser, 8th September 1906
[6] The Daily Gazette, 6th October 1879
[7] Yorkshire Post and Leeds Intelligencer, 20 January 1880
[8] The Daily Gazette, 19th January 1880
[9] Sheffield Daily Telegraph, 8th November 1880
[10] Stockton Herald, South Durham and Cleveland Advertiser, 8th September 1906
[11] Yorkshire Post and Leeds Intelligencer, 3rd January 1881
[12] The York Herald, 14th February 1881
[13] Yorkshire Post and Leeds Intelligencer, 8th March 1881
[14] The York Herald, 29th May 1882
[15] The York Herald, 24th October 1881
[16] Newcastle Journal, 6th March 1882
[17] The York Herald, 6th March 1882
[18] The Liverpool Mercury, 13th March 1882
[19] The York Herald, 13th March 1882
[20] The York Herald, 3rd April 1882
[21] Newcastle Journal, 3rd April 1882
[22] Green 'Un, 4th April 1914
[23] The York Herald, 5th December 1881
[24] Sheffield and Rotherham Independent, 14th November 1881
[25] Bucks Herald, 19th November 1881
[26] Nottingham Evening Post, 30th January 1882
[27] The York Herald, 9th October 1882
[28] Nottingham Evening Post, 13th February 1883
[29] Sheffield Daily Telegraph, 11th December 1883
[30] The York Herald, 5th March 1883
[31] The Leeds Mercury, 26th March 1883
[32] Sheffield and Rotherham Independent, 15th October 1883
[33] Sheffield Daily Telegraph, 16th October 1883
[34] The North Eastern Weekly Gazette, 27th October 1883
[35] The Athletic News, 5th December 1883
[36] The York Herald, 7th April 1884
[37] The North Eastern Daily Gazette, 19th April 1884
[38] The Sheffield Daily Telegraph, 23rd December 1884
[39] The Wednesday Boys, Jason Dickinson and John Brodie
[40] The York Herald, 10th November 1884
[41] The Sunderland Echo, 11th November 1884

[42] The Lincolnshire Chronicle, 9th December 1883
[43] The Field, 13th December 1884
[44] The North Eastern Weekly Gazette, 22nd November 1884
[45] The North Eastern Weekly Gazette, 29th November 1884
[46] Yorkshire Gazette, 16th March 1885
[47] Yorkshire Evening Press, 16th March 1885
[48] The Northern Echo, 17th March 1885
[49] The North Eastern Daily Gazette, 12th February 1885
[50] The North Eastern Weekly Gazette, 28th March 1885
[51] The North Eastern Weekly Gazette, 27th October, 1883
[52] The Northern Echo, 25th January 1886
[53] The Athletic News, 16th February 1886
[54] The Sporting Life, 15th February 1886
[55] The Sportsman, 15th February 1886
[56] The Athletic News, 24th February 1890
[57] The Northern Echo, 15th November 1886
[58] The Northern Echo, 20th November 1886
[59] The Northern Echo, 23rd November 1886
[60] Saltburn Times, 30th September 1887
[61] Northern Review, 1st January 1887
[62] The York Herald, 24th September 1887
[63] Northern Review, 12th November 1887
[64] The Athletic News, 11th January 1887
[65] Northern Review, 5th February 1886
[66] Northern Review, 12th February 1887
[67] Northern Review, 26th November 1887
[68] The Sheffield and Rotherham Independent, 6th October 1888
[69] Yorkshire Evening Press, 11th February 1889
[70] Northern Echo, 2nd March 1889
[71] Northern Echo, 11th March 1889
[72] The Sheffield Telegraph, 8th October 1888
[73] The North Eastern Daily Gazette, 31st August 1889
[74] The North Eastern Daily Gazette, 28th February 1889
[75] https://www.cdc.gov/tb/worldtbday/history.htm
[76] James E. Pollock, "Considerations of the Climate of Italy", London Medical Gazette 11 (1850): 1017; Hoolihan, "Health and Travel", 468.
[77] "South Africa, Orange Free State, Probate Records from the Master of the Supreme Court, 1832-1989," database, *FamilySearch* (https://familysearch.org/ark:/61903/3:1:3QS7-89LW-K7XM?cc=3040532 : 24 August 2019), > image 1 of 1; citing Master's Office of the Orange Free State Archives, Bloemfontein.
[78] The Evening Telegraph and Star, 23rd April 1890
[79] Morpeth Herald, 26th October 1889
[80] Newcastle Daily Chronicle, 17th June 1890
[81] Newcastle Daily Chronicle, 19th May 1890
[82] https://www.visionofbritain.org.uk/

[83] The North Eastern Weekly Gazette, 18th May 1889
[84] The Northern Echo, 5th March 1890
[85] Daily Gazette for Middlesbrough, 18th March 1890
[86] The Redcar and Saltburn-by-the-Sea Gazette, 19th April 1890
[87] The Athletic News, 2nd October 1911
[88] Northern Weekly Gazette, 22nd March 1890
[89] Daily Gazette for Middlesbrough, 5th October 1894
[90] The York Herald, 9th October 1894
[91] Green 'Un, 4th April 1914
[92] Stockton Herald, South Durham and Cleveland Advertiser, 8th September 1906
[93] The Northern Echo, 23rd April 1900
[94] Sheffield Daily Telegraph, 9th March 1903
[95] Athletic News, 13th November 1905
[96] Star Green 'un, 6th January 1912
[97] Newcastle Journal, 3rd August 1943
[98] Hartlepool Northern Daily Mail, 3rd August 1943
[99] Stockton Herald, South Durham and Cleveland Advertiser, 8th September 1906
[100] Star Green 'un, The Week and Sports Special, 17th January 1914
[101] Hartlepool Northern Daily Mail, 16th April 1908
[102] Star Green 'Un, Football and Sports Special, 3rd April 1909
[103] Star Green 'un, 24th April 1909
[104] Leeds Mercury, 28th May 1909
[105] Daily Gazette for Middlesbrough, 18th August 1913
[106] North Eastern Daily Gazette, 22nd July 1913
[107] The Yorkshire Post, 8th September 1913
[108] Sports Gazette, 20th September 1913
[109] Sports Gazette, 27th September 1913
[110] Sports Gazette, 6th December 1913
[111] Sports Gazette, 13th December 1913
[112] The Newcastle Daily Chronicle, 29th December 1913
[113] Daily Gazette for Middlesbrough, 9th January 1914
[114] Sports Gazette, 24th January 1914
[115] Daily Gazette for Middlesbrough, 2nd February 1914
[116] Sports Gazette, 14th February 1914
[117] Green 'Un, 4th April 1914
[118] Daily Gazette for Middlesbrough, 3rd April 1914
[119] Daily Gazette for Middlesbrough, 17th April 1914
[120] Sports Gazette, 15th April 1914
[121] Daily Gazette for Middlesbrough, 27th June 1914
[122] Sports Gazette, 17th May 1919
[123] Yorkshire Post and Leeds Intelligencer, 22nd September 1919
[124] Yorkshire Post and Leeds Intelligencer, 12th January 1920
[125] Leeds Mercury, 29th January 1919
[126] Sports Gazette, 20th May 1920
[127] Daily Gazette for Middlesbrough, 29th September 1920
[128] Daily Gazette for Middlesbrough, 29th September 1920

[129] Daily Gazette for Middlesbrough, 23rd November 1920
[130] Yorkshire Post and Leeds Intelligencer, 27th September 1920
[131] Sports Gazette, 16th April 1921
[132] Northern Goalfields, Brian Hunt
[133] The Athletic News, 21st February 1921
[134] Sports Gazette, 28th August 1921
[135] Sports Gazette, 17th September 1921
[136] Sports Gazette, 24th September 1921
[137] Sports Gazette, 12th November 1921
[138] Sports Gazette, 31st December 1921
[139] Sports Gazette, 22nd February 1922
[140] Sports Gazette, 10th March 1923
[141] Morecambe Guardian, 23rd September 1922
[142] Leeds Mercury, 24th October 1922
[143] Athletic News, 10th August 1925
[144] Sports Gazette, 16th April 1921
[145] Derby Telegraph, 7th January 1928
[146] The Athletic News, 16th February 1925
[147] Sports Gazette, 21st February 1925
[148] Sports Gazette, 14th February 1925
[149] The Athletic News, 16th February 1925
[150] Sports Gazette, 11th April 1922
[151] Liverpool Echo, 17th March 1934
[152] Daily Gazette for Middlesbrough, 5th May 1934
[153] Sports Gazette, 2nd December 1933
[154] Sports Gazette, 20th October 1934
[155] Sports Gazette, 10th November 1934
[156] Sports Gazette, 17th November 1934
[157] Sports Gazette, 8th December 1934
[158] Evening Gazette, 22nd November 1940
[159] Evening Gazette, 30th December 1940
[160] https://www.wlv.ac.uk/
[161] Daily Mirror, 5th March 1954
[162] Daily Herald, 8th March 1954
[163] https://www.horshamfc.co.uk/matches/1956-57/12724/chelsea-a-venue-unknown/
[164] http://watfordfcarchive.co.uk/
[165] Sunday People, 4th December 1960
[166] Western Mail, 22nd December 1955
[167] Whitby Town vs Redcar Albion programme, 17th November 1956
[168] Northern Daily Mail, 19th June 1958
[169] https://www.whitbytownfc.com/news/jackie-boltons-time-at-whitby-town--part-1-2535318.html
[170] Redcar Albion vs Durham City programme, 23rd November 1957
[171] Penrith Observer, 5th June 1956
[172] Evening Gazette, 4th September 1962

[173] The Journal, 27th April 1960
[174] Evening Gazette, 30th April 1960
[175] Evening Gazette, 30th April 1960
[176] Evening Gazette, n.d. February 1963
[177] When I Write My Book! by Mal Bean
[178] Stockton Herald, South Durham and Cleveland Advertiser, 8th September 1906
[179] Redcar Albion vs Eppleton Colliery Welfare programme, 14th November 1981
[180] Football Annual 1880-1889, CW Alcock
[181] Redcar Albion membership booklet 1960-70

Front cover images, clockwise from top left:
Lawrie Crown - Courtesy of P Joannou Archive
William Harrison – Courtesy of Sheffield Wednesday Football Club
Bobby Smith – Courtesy of Joyce Charlesworth
Tim Williamson – Singleton and Cole's Cigarettes, 1905
James Howcroft – Sports Picture Post, n.d. 1912
Jack Bolton – Courtesy of Gary and Jack Bolton